NORTHERN IRELAND AND THE ALGERIAN ANALOGY

OTHER ATHOL BOOKS PUBLICATIONS

The Life And Poems Of Thomas Moore

The Veto Controversy including Thomas Moore's
Letter To The Roman Catholics Of Dublin (1810)
Compiled by Brendan Clifford
(Extracts from the dispute within Irish Catholicism which was a watershed in Irish political development, and which resulted in the subordination of the state to the Church in nationalist Ireland, and in the Partition of Ireland.)

The Birth Of Ulster Unionism
(The United Irishmen; the Arian Controversy; the Agrarian Revolution; the Home Rule Bill)

On the Anglo-Irish Agreement:
Parliamentary Sovereignty And Northern Ireland,
A Review Of The Party System In The British Constitution, With Relation To The Anglo-Irish Agreement, by Brendan Clifford

Parliamentary Despotism, John Hume's Aspiration
by Brendan Clifford

Integration, A Word Without Meaning
by Jim Davidson

A Full List of BEVIN SOCIETY Publications can be had from the Secretary at the address overleaf.

NORTHERN IRELAND AND THE ALGERIAN ANALOGY

A Suitable Case For Gaullism?

Athol Books
and
The Bevin Society

PUBLISHED BY

Athol Books, 10 Athol Street, Belfast, BT12 4GX

in conjunction with

The Bevin Society: Secretary, Hugh Roberts,
114 Lordship Road, London, N16.

ISBN 0 85034 031 4

© ATHOL BOOKS 1986

This book is sold subject to the condition that
it shall not, by way of trade or otherwise, be
lent, resold, hired out, or otherwise circulated
without the publisher's prior consent in any
form of binding or cover other than that in
which it is published and without a similar condition including this condition being imposed
on the subsequent purchaser.

Contents

Foreword, by Robert McCartney	Page 7
The Colonial Assumption	Page 9
The Anglo-Irish Agreement	Page 11
Knowledge, Pseudo-Knowledge And Analogy	Page 17
Analogies, Popular And Unpopular	Page 18
Baroness Ewart-Biggs	Page 20
The Prophet: R.W. Johnson	Page 21
Johnson's Format And Premise	Page 22
Johnson On "Terrorism"	Page 23
Irish Nationalism's Double Act, Or The Uses Of Humbug	Page 25
Whose Consent Is It Anyway?	Page 26
Consent And The South	Page 31
Bad History	Page 32
"A Matter Of Geography"	Page 35
Catholicism, Islam And Tolerance	Page 38
Church And State	Page 41
The French In Algeria	Page 47
The Protestants In Ulster	Page 51
Settlers And Natives In Algeria	Page 56
Settlers And Natives In Ireland	Page 60
Conclusion	Page 67
Appendix	Page 69
Biographical Note On Hugh Roberts	Page 70

Foreword

The almost universal ignorance of the British ruling class of Ireland, its people and their ways of thought strengthened their tendency to regard Ireland as a half alien dependency. So wrote J.C. Beckett, one of Ireland's most distinguished historians, of British attitudes to Ireland after the Act of Union of 1800. Almost two hundred years later little has changed. The signing of the Anglo-Irish Agreement and the manner in which Northern Ireland has been governed since 1921 and particularly since 1972 confirm that the same ignorance and attitude are just as entrenched.

Hugh Roberts' lucid and compelling paper lays bare the plethora of false assumptions and questionable comparisons which litter the thinking and politics of the British political, academic and media establishment. The comparison between the French experience in Algeria and British policy in Northern Ireland could not have been better chosen to demonstrate the welter of flawed reasoning, superficial analysis and deliberate analogical bias in many of the arguments mounted against the fundamental claim of the clear majority in Northern Ireland to enjoy full equality of citizenship and full expression of their rights of franchise and political liberty within the United Kingdom of Great Britain and Northern Ireland.

The wealth of detailed knowledge, sensitive perceptions and careful analyses which has been brought to bear upon the comparison of the Algerian and Northern Ireland situations brilliantly exposes the dangers of the simple comparisons so attractive to either the intellectually lazy or incompetent and so easily potted by a like-minded media.

The fundamental difference between the French Algerian colon and the Ulster Unionist is clearly illustrated. Not only does the Ulster Unionist form a substantial majority in Northern Ireland which the colon never did in Algeria, but his relationship with the Catholic minority was totally different from the colons with the Muslim majority. On another level the basic differences between the French and British attitudes to the state and its mode of government are lucidly expounded, as well as the truism that differences between religions are often more easily tolerated than heresies within. Hugh Roberts endorses with inimitable style the view of political geographers that the theory of natural boundaries should not only be rejected, but the term banned from scientific literature. One wonders why a concept so beloved by the fascist dictators should be so heavily endorsed by the British left in their support for a United Ireland.

The range of argument and depth of scholarship take the paper well beyond the confines of its title, and Hugh Roberts rightly concludes that the Unionists of Ulster are no mere colonial caste without rights or beliefs. Ulster Unionists are of the same stock as the founding fathers of the United States and as British as Maragaret Thatcher's Finchley electorate. Only when the British establishment and political parties become informed enough to start treating them as such will a solution to the Northern Ireland problem become a reality. This paper is a major contribution to that informative process, for which my fellow British citizens in Northern Ireland will remain deeply grateful.

Robert McCartney
May 1986

The Colonial Assumption

The idea that Northern Ireland is a British colony has been implicit in the attitude of the British political establishment as a whole since the passing of the Government Of Ireland Act in 1920. It was by no means universal before this date. The Independent Labour Party, for instance, regularly contested elections in what is now Northern Ireland before the First World War, and polled very respectably in the working class districts of Belfast. But since the Partition of Ireland, the collective refusal of the British political parties to accept members from Northern Ireland or to contest elections there has rested in large part on the tacit assumption, inherited from Gladstone, that Northern Ireland is an integral part of Ireland rather than of the British state, and that its actual constitutional position within the United Kingdom is an awkward historical anomaly.

This attitude has made it exceptionally difficult, in fact, psychologically impossible, for British politicians to rebut the irredentist claims of the Irish Republic. While repeatedly paying lip-service to the democratic principle that Northern Ireland is entitled to remain within the United Kingdom for as long as its population so wish, British politicians have never at any stage publicly contested the claim to sovereignty over the North expressed in Articles 2 and 3 of the Republic of Ireland's Constitution. At no point in the last sixteen years, while the war has raged in Northern Ireland, has the British government even considered referring the matter of this disputed sovereignty to the International Court of Justice at The Hague, although similar disputes are regularly referred to it by other countries. Instead, an elaborate pretence has been maintained that the South's claim is not to be taken seriously, that it does not mean anything, it is all merely holy writ — and why make a fuss about holy writ if it does not mean anything? Unfortunately, it does mean something. And it is taken very seriously by certain people, the Provisional IRA for a start, but also the courts in Eire. The Sunningdale Agreement of 1973 foundered on these articles of the Republic's Constitution, when it was discovered that the Taoiseach, Liam Cosgrave, had conceded more than he was constitutionally entitled to do — all this long before the Ulster Workers' strike of 1974. But the British government has preferred to turn a blind eye to this evidence of the significance of the South's claim to sovereignty. This can hardly be unconnected with the fact that much of the British political establishment is inclined to regard this claim as a legitimate one, and to regard the British position in Northern Ireland as embarrassing rather than legitimate.

From 1920 to 1972, Northern Ireland was obliged to operate a form of devolved government which kept it at arm's length from the political life of the rest of the United Kingdom, a system which was imposed on the province against the wishes of the Ulster Unionist leaders, who predicted with complete accuracy what its result would be: the institutionalisation and perpetuation of sectarianism. From 1972 onwards, the province has been governed directly from Westminster, but in a manner which has in no way resembled the way in which Scotland or Wales are governed, for the simple but fundamental reason that Northern Ireland has continued to be excluded from the party system upon which representative democracy in the rest of the United Kingdom has been based since the days of the Whigs and Tories. The Northern Ireland Office has functioned exactly like a colonial administration and the Northern Ireland Secretary like a Viceroy. At Westminster, legislation concerning Northern Ireland has been an affair of Orders in Council, and hence not subject to the normal processes of Parliamentary scrutiny and debate which are standard in all other matters.

Since the dissolution of Stormont in 1972, the policy of successive British governments has boiled down to the endeavour to persuade the *"natives"* of the colony to sink their differences sufficiently to permit Westminster to wash its hands of the place once more. Repeated attempts have been made to re-establish devolved government, without success. The idea of an Independent Ulster was vigorously canvassed by the Northern Ireland Office under Merlyn Rees in 1974-5, with the support of The Times and a section of the British Marxist intelligentsia (Tom Nairn, of the New Left Review clique). And now the concept of an Anglo-Irish condominium — or, rather, of an Anglo-Irish joint protectorate, previously resisted by sections of the Conservative Party, including Mrs. Thatcher, has been adopted *faute de mieux*.

What all these formulae have in common is the assumption that Northern Ireland is not an integral part of the United Kindgom, but a place apart, for which special arrangements need to be made, whether these enjoy the consent of its population or not. The one option which the British political establishment has consistently refused to contemplate is that of integration, of treating Northern Ireland like any other region of the United Kingdom, allowing its population to participate fully in the normal, healthy, democratic political life of the state as a whole and thereby evolve out of the sectarian impasse to which it was condemned in 1920. It has been an article of faith amongst British politicians that the people of Northern Ireland are incorrigibly sectarian, that sectarianism is an immutable because intrinsic element of their nature. While frequently bemoaning the *"tribal"* behaviour of the Northern Irish, British politicians have in fact used this behaviour to justify their own refusal to have anything to do with the place.

These frankly racist attitudes on the part of the British political establishment are the ideological counterpart of a consistently colonial approach to the Northern Ireland problem. This colonial approach has done anything but produce a solution to the problem. Misconceiving the problem, it has produced only misconceived "*solutions*" to it. And by sustaining their collective boycott of the province, the British political parties have succeeded in permanently insulating themselves from the realities of Northern Ireland, and have thereby preserved their misconceptions intact.

All this has, of course, been grist to the mill of Irish Republicanism, for which the Anglo-Irish Agreement represents a remarkable victory, although by no means a decisive one. The only element of the British political establishment which has historically been disposed to resist the irredentist claims of the Irish Republic as a matter of principle, the Thatcher wing of the Conservative Party, has capitulated at last. It cannot seriously be supposed that the Anglo-Irish Agreement is a formula for restoring political stability to the province within the United Kingdom. It is without question a stepping stone to a United Ireland, in so far as it is a formula designed to revive and enhance the prospect of eventual unification. And it assumes that the Protestants of Northern Ireland can be dealt with in the same way as de Gaulle dealt with the "*colons*" of French Algeria.

In other words, the British political establishment, whether wittingly or not, has at last begun to follow to the end the logic of its own colonialist assumptions, and the moment of truth for those assumptions is at hand.

The Anglo-Irish Agreement

Not the least remarkable thing about the Anglo-Irish Agreement is the fact that nobody on the mainland (apart from a few principled Conservative MPs) appears to have read it. The leader-writers of Fleet Street most certainly have not read it. Tom King has probably got around to reading it by now, but he certainly did not know what it contained in the first week or two after it was signed. He thought it contained an acknowledgement by Dublin that "*in practical terms and in perpetuity*" there could not be a United Ireland, a thought he expressed aloud in Brussels. The resulting uproar in Dublin made it very clear that it contained nothing of the sort, and we were presented with the extraordinary spectacle of the Secretary of State for Northern Ireland who had just been involved in negotiating an agreement apologising in the House of Commons for having misinterpreted that agreement.

But it was not only poor old Tom King who got it wrong. When Mrs. Thatcher was opening the Debate on the Agreement in the House of Commons on November 26, 1985, she too did not fully understand what she was recommending to the House. In an interview in the Belfast Telegraph on December 17, 1985, she declared that *"the people of Northern Ireland can get rid of the Intergovernmental Conference by agreeing to devolved government"*. This is simply untrue. The Agreement which sets up the Intergovernmental Conference in no way provides for this Conference to be dissolved as soon as the people of Northern Ireland reach agreement on devolved government. Once again, the British government has had to be called to order by Dublin. The Unionists can make whatever concessions on power-sharing they like to John Hume and the SDLP, this will not get rid of the Intergovernmental Conference at all. That this is indeed the true position was, at long last, made very clear by Tom King in an interview with Sir Robin Day on the BBC programme, "The World At One", on February 25, 1986.

An agreement with a foreign government has been recommended to the House of Commons by a Prime Minister and a Secretary of State who neither of them properly understood what they were recommending. It was endorsed by a majority of 473 to 47, after a two-day debate in which the most cogent objections by the Ulster Unionist MPs and certain Conservative backbenchers went entirely unanswered. It can safely be said that the vast majority of the 473 MPs who voted in support of the Agreement neither knew what they were voting for, nor cared. None of them have any Northern Ireland constituents to worry about, after all.

It may be said that the British Government's intentions in negotiating this Agreement were entirely honourable and that the purpose of the Agreement is to restore peace and stability to Northern Ireland by enlisting the cooperation of the Irish government in this endeavour. But governments come and go. It is not the subjective intentions of Mrs. Thatcher or Garret FitzGerald that matter, it is the terms and implications of a formal Agreement which has been registered with the United Nations. This Agreement recognises the right of the Irish government to represent the Catholic community in Northern Ireland in the regular meetings of the Intergovernmental Conference (Article 5 (c)). This right has not been democratically bestowed on the Irish government by the Catholic community and the Irish government is in no way accountable to the Catholics of Northern Ireland for the manner in which it represents them. The Agreement in effect allows the Irish government to establish a quasi-protectorate over the Catholic community in the North. Why should such a concession have been necessary in order to secure Dublin's cooperation in the fight against the IRA?

To suppose that the Agreement will prove to be a formula for political stability in Northern Ireland is to assume either that the Provisional IRA will be satisfied with the Anglo-Irish joint protectorate which has been established, and will accordingly call off its military campaign, or that, irrespective of the IRA's private sentiments in the matter, the Irish government is in a position to induce it to settle, once and for all, for half a loaf. There is absolutely no ground whatever' for either of these assumptions. Having sustained a sixteen-year military campaign with remarkable tactical skill, the IRA cannot seriously be expected to abandon its activities once these have at last begun to bear fruit. To suppose that the Irish Government is able to induce it to do so is to suppose that the Irish Government has substantial authority over the Provisional IRA Army Council, or that it has been seriously pulling its punches in its security operations against the IRA since 1970 and has only to act decisively against the IRA to put an end to it once and for all. But is this what Garret FitzGerald would have us believe?

Unless it is successfully resisted, the Anglo-Irish Agreement can function only as a device for setting Northern Ireland irrevocably upon the road to incorporation within the Irish Republic. These are not the terms in which it has been presented by spokesmen for the British Government, but they are the terms in which it is being widely presented in Southern Ireland. And many Labour MPs known for their Republican sympathies voted for the Agreement in the House of Commons on November 27, 1985 on these grounds. The Agreement represents a fundamental and far-reaching concession by the British Government to the irredentist claims of the Irish Republic, as expressed in Articles 2 and 3 of the Republic's Constitution. The Republic has conceded nothing of substance in return. Vague noises about increased cross-border cooperation mean little. The recently announced decision to sign the European Convention on Terrorism also means little. (And why, we are entitled to ask, has it taken the Republic over 9 years to get around to this?) This decision was given a vigorous trumpeting by the media, but it does not remove the main obstacle to the extradition of IRA and INLA terrorists wanted for offences committed in the North, which is the Republic's view that these are *"political"* in nature and therefore non-extraditable under Eire's 1965 Extradition Act. Garret FitzGerald has expressed the intention to bring in new legislation *"in the present year"* (1986) to supercede the 1965 Act, but the form of this legislation has yet to be decided. It could be years before the Republic's signing of the European Convention has any practical effect on IRA or INLA activities.

The only concession the Republic could have made which would seriously have contributed to the restoration of peace and stability in the North was to have dropped Articles 2 and 3 of its Constitution. This would have greatly weakened the propaganda position of the IRA and would have gone a long way towards convincing the Protestants that the constitutional status of Northern Ireland was indeed secure at last. But as anyone who bothers to follow Southern Irish politics will be aware, it was emphasised in the debate on the Agreement in the Dail that the Agreement did not in any way retract the claim to *de jure* sovereignty over the North which is asserted in Article 2 of the Constitution. It merely expressed the Irish Government's recognition of the empirical fact that it does not actually enjoy *de facto* sovereignty. But this has always been the position of the Irish government since De Valera abrogated the Agreement signed by the Government of the Free State in 1925, in which the legitimacy of the constitutional status of Northern Ireland was unequivocally acknowledged, for the first and last time. Dick Spring, the leader of the Irish Labour Party who is Garret FitzGerald's deputy leader (Tanaiste) in the Coalition Government, took pains to set the Dail's mind at rest on this score:

"Regarding the recognition of the State of Northern Ireland by that move, he said, all politicians since the foundation of the state had recognised the factual situation. Nothing changes in that regard, and nothing changes in regard to our Constitution either" (Irish Times, November 16, 1985).

Whether out of stupidity or duplicity or absent-mindedness, Mrs. Thatcher and Douglas Hurd (who, as Tom King's predecessor, was the principal British negotiator of the Agreement) have deliberately done Garret FitzGerald's and John Hume's bidding. They have outflanked *"the Loyalist veto"*, as the fashionable double-talk would have it. In plain English, they have reneged on the principle that there should be no change in the constitutional status of Northern Ireland without the consent of the people of Northern Ireland.

The government of the Republic has been accorded a regular, institutionalised and far-reaching say in the government of Northern Ireland. This is officially described in the Republic as a *"less than executive"* but *"more than consultative role"*. (The claim in The Sunday Times on March 9, 1986 that the Agreement *"allows Dublin to be consulted on aspects of Ulster's affairs"* must surely beat all comers in the understatement championship of 1986. But it will have plenty of competition. The performance of the British media on this issue has simply beggared belief.) In reality, it has been given a joint *de facto* legislative role, in view of the extent to which Parliament has already abdicated in practice its legislative responsibilities with regard to Northern Ireland by the operation of the Orders in Council system. In effect, the Intergovernmental Conference will take policy decisions on Northern Ireland on all matters of importance and these will be rubber-stamped by the British Parliament. The text of the Agreement specifically mentions:

> *(i) political matters;*
> *(ii) security and related matters;*
> *(iii) legal matters, including the administration of justice;*
> *(iv) the promotion of cross-border cooperation".*

Nowhere in the text of the Agreement is *"political"* defined. It should not take more than a moment's thought to realise that a very wide range of questions can quite reasonably be considered to be *"political"* in Northern Ireland, from state funding of independent schools to housing policy and the siting of new industries. The Agreement provides no clear limit whatever to the range of issues on which the Irish government may make its views known.

It is nothing less than a lie to state that the Intergovernmental Conference is merely a forum for the purpose of *"consulting"* the Irish government. The text of the Agreement does not speak in terms of **"consulting"** at all. It specifically says that the Intergovernmental Conference has been set up *"to deal...on a regular basis with"* the matters listed under i-iv above (emphasis added). Moreover, Article 2 (b) states that

> *"The United Kingdom Government accept that the Irish Government will put forward views and proposals on matters relating to Northern Ireland... determined efforts shall be made through the Conference to resolve any differences".*

The role of the Irish government is therefore not to be a passive object of consultation. It will have an active role. And the British government is obliged by the terms of an Agreement now registered at the United Nations to do everything in its power to reach agreement with the representatives of the Irish government on the proposals they put forward.

It may be said that this is a far-fetched reading of the clause in question. In fact, it is merely a realistic reading. Tom King's reading of Article 1, for which he got into so much hot water last December, was by no means an unreasonable reading. But it was not Dublin's reading. Not the least significant feature of the Agreement is the studied vagueness of much of its text. What does *"deal with"* mean? What does *"political"* mean? The greatest imprecision has been employed where the employment of precision would seem to have been a prerequisite of securing general acceptance for the Agreement in Northern Ireland. But there is nothing imprecise about the obligation of the British government to make *"determined efforts...to resolve any differences"*. It will not be possible for Tom King to listen politely to whatever Peter Barry may come up with and then simply say with a sweet smile, *"Sorry, old boy, it is just not on"*. Dublin has already made clear on two occasions its determination to ensure that its interpretation of the Agreement prevails. It can be counted on to do so in future, should the need arise. The imprecision of the terminology employed has undoubtedly been deliberate. It gives a very large amount of *carte blanche* to Dublin. And its political implications cannot be calculated.

This major constitutional change has been enacted without any consultation of the people of Northern Ireland, with one exception. John Hume and the leadership of the Social Democratic and Labour Party were consulted throughout, and it cannot seriously be doubted that Hume had a large part in the drafting of the Agreement. But the elected representatives of the Unionist majority were totally excluded from the talks which produced the Agreement. The British Government has refused, moreover, to submit the Agreement to a referendum, although the far less radical constitutional changes in the proposals for devolution in Scotland and Wales were submitted to referenda in Scotland and Wales, and the Scottish and Welsh populations were granted, as of right, a final say in the matter. And when the people of Northern Ireland registered their overwhelming opposition to the Agreement in the by-elections of January 23, 1986, Tom King made clear the Government's determination to discount and override this opposition. The very fact that this massive opposition was predictable was cited as grounds for ignoring it.

The principle of consent has been flouted in the most flagrant and thorough-going way. It has been flouted not only by the British Government, but by all the mainland British political parties whose members voted for the Agreement on November 27, 1985. It has been flouted, in particular, by the Parliamentary Labour Party, whose members, in supporting the Agreement, were simultaneously flouting their own party's policy, by which the party is committed to the principle of consent as the precondition of constitutional change. The Parliamentary Labour Party's decision to support the Agreement was taken in the most casual way imaginable. The Labour Party NEC did not even discuss the Agreement at its November 1985 meeting.

The flouting of the principle of consent is a fact. No amount of humbugging lip-service to this principle by those who have flouted it can change this fact. And it assumes that this principle can be flouted with impunity. It assumes that the opponents of the Agreement in Northern Ireland will turn out to be men of straw. There can be no doubt that this is exactly what the architects and supporters of the Agreement take them for. They expect the Protestants of Northern Ireland to suffer a terminal collapse of will once the writing is finally and unmistakeably on the wall. They expect them to behave like *"colons* and, as is well known, *"colons"* invariably turn out to be men of straw once their bluff is called.

Knowledge, Pseudo-Knowledge And Analogy

The Protestant community in Northern Ireland is not made up of men, or women, of straw nor is it a community of *"colons"*. But in England, and in particular in those circles of the political, intellectual and media establishments which have so unanimously welcomed the Agreement, it is widely supposed that it is. This supposition is a misapprehension founded upon ignorance. In the case of many people, it is undoubtedly a sincere and genuine misapprehension. But the ignorance upon which it is founded is inexcusable.

A murderous little war has been going on in Northern Ireland for the last sixteen years. A political establishment worth its salt would have made it its business to investigate and acquaint itself with the true character of the protagonists of this war long ago. The ignorance of the political establishment is inexcusable because it has been a wilful ignorance. But the establishment is quite incapable of recognising how perversely ignorant it has been. It is a necessary feature of the collective self-image of *"the great and the good"*, as the members of the establishment like to think of themselves, that they are the ones in the know. Sophistication is their stock-in-trade. It is upon their virtual monopoly of sophistication that they base their claims to the interesting and well-remunerated positions in public life which they have secured for themselves. They sustain this congenial state of affairs by virtue of the fact that they are themselves the arbiters of what passes for sophistication. And, in relation to Northern Ireland, they conceal and compensate for their profound and wilful ignorance by drawing from a seemingly bottomless well of sophisticated pseudo-knowledge.

The most important element of this stock of pseudo-knowledge has been a collection of arguments by analogy.

Analogies certainly have their place in political analysis. By comparing two or more situations which are analogous in important respects, and identifying the ways in which they differ, one can arrive at a deeper understanding of the situations in question. A sociologist, concerned to develop some general theory, may be uninterested in the differences between such cases. But for the practical politician, it is precisely the differences between otherwise analogous situations which will matter, for politics deals with an unending series of unique situations. It is only powerful dictatorships which may ride roughshod over the complexities of reality.

But analogies are no substitute for investigation and experience. They may usefully be employed only when the primary case under study has been fully explored in its own terms. Those who neglect this elementary rule will not acquire or produce knowledge of the primary case, but pseudo-knowledge, pretentious clap-trap masquerading as knowledge.

Analogies, Popular And Unpopular

At least five different analogies have been deployed at regular intervals with regard to Northern Ireland by those hostile to the Union. These are the analogies with the Civil Rights movement in the United States in the 1960s, the Israel-Arab conflict in Palestine, Rhodesia, South Africa and Algeria. Other analogies which have been at least as pertinent, if not more so, have been systematically overlooked because of their inconvenient implications from the Irish Republican point of view; these include the case of Alsace-Lorraine, of the Saar, of the Sudetenland, the Kosovo region of Yugoslavia, inhabited by ethnic Albanians, and the partition of India.

The front-runner initially was the analogy with the Civil Rights movement in the United States. This was extremely popular with the English intelligentsia in the late 1960s, dazzled as it was by things American in general and the Kennedy phenomenon in particular. The fact that the Catholic community in Northern Ireland was there of its own free will, had never been enslaved, was not the object of any legislative discrimination or enforced segregation whatever and enjoyed full political rights was simply neither here nor there. (Apart from the gerrymandering of a couple of constituency boundaries in the local, though not in the Westminster, Elections, the one measure of discrimination which the Northern Ireland Civil Rights Association was able to point to, the property qualification on the local government franchise, did not discriminate against Catholics but applied equally to Protestants, and actually affected more Protestants than Catholics.)

Had this analogy been accurate, the troubles in Northern Ireland would have ended fourteen years ago, if not earlier. The grievances raised by NICRA were dealt with in the reforms enacted by Stormont in 1969 and 1970. And the argument that these were purely formal changes and that the apparatus of Protestant oppression remained intact, although disingenuous at best, became entirely obsolete when Stormont was itself abolished in 1972. Yet, as we all know, this did not end the matter. The IRA launched its war at precisely the moment when the NICRA was achieving its stated goals. To suggest that the substance of the Northern Ireland problem has been a question of civil rights is absurd. The insurrectionary separatism of the Black Panthers was an ephemeral and superficial aspect of the movement for civil rights in the American Black community (and was accordingly heavily patronised by white *"liberals"* in the heyday of Radical Chic). But the relationship between insurrectionary separatism and civil rights campaigning in Northern Ireland has been the exact opposite of the American case. The substance of the Catholic mobilisation in Northern Ireland has been the Republican separatist offensive against Partition. John Hume's SDLP has been as integral a part of that offensive as the Provisional IRA. *"Constitutional nationalism"* is still nationalism. The original founders of the NICRA, the McCluskeys, very possibly took their movement's stated goals in earnest. But who remembers their names today? For practically everybody else, the civil rights issue was simply grist to the nationalist mill. But Martin Luther King is not forgotten, and it can confidently be stated that he will not be forgotten for a very long time to come, because he represented and articulated the substance of what was at issue in the United States in the 1960s.

It is precisely because they have been well aware of the weakness of the analogy with the Black civil rights movement in America that many members of the British intelligentsia and political establishment have resorted to other analogies: Israel, South Africa, White Rhodesia and so forth. All these analogies have their virtues. They all provide short-cuts, like the civil rights analogy, enabling people to work out their *"position"* on Northern Ireland by formal deduction, transferring sympathies and judgements developed in other contexts to the Northern Ireland situation without thinking. That is a very great advantage, of course. They also contain two essential ingedients, as did the civil rights analogy: a people whose cause one can patronise, and a people whom one can slander and damn with a clear conscience. For the arbiters of political taste and fashion who make up such a large proportion of *"the great and the good"*, such things are not trifles or luxuries, they are the air they breathe, their daily bread and butter.

But each of these analogies has its drawbacks. Northern Ireland is not an independent state like Israel or South Africa or, for that matter, Rhodesia after UDI. The Catholic-Protestant ratio in Northern Ireland bears no relation to the black-white ratio in Rhodesia or South Africa. In neither the South African nor the Rhodesian cases have blacks enjoyed the right to vote and take part in the political life of the state, as the Catholics of Northern Ireland have. And is the PLO regularly allowed to contest elections in Israel? One could go on, multiplying such discrepancies between these putative analogies and the most elementary aspects of political reality in Northern Ireland.

There is another analogy, however, which has enjoyed an intermittent popularity with English politicians and intellectuals, and which is now coming to the fore once more. This is the analogy with Algeria. It has been put forward most recently by Baroness Ewart-Biggs, widow of the British ambassador to Dublin whom the IRA murdered some years ago, who is now a Labour peeress. But it has also been actively canvassed, if only by implication, by the very clever and undoubtedly influential commentator, Brian

Walden in his column in the London Standard (December 10, 1985). And it was stated in the most uninhibited manner by another fashionable and influential political commentator, R.W. Johnson, Fellow in Politics at Magdalen College, Oxford, in an article in his regular New Society column on June 25, 1981, republished in his collected essays, **The Politics Of Recession**, in 1985.

These are not negligible figures in the British political and intellectual establishment. On the contrary, they are representative of a substantial and influential current of opinion within it. And because they none of them hold positions of political responsibility, they are free to state the true rationale of government policy towards Northern Ireland far more coherently and frankly than would be expedient for the actual architects or official executants of this policy.

Baroness Ewart-Biggs

Speaking in the Debate on the Anglo-Irish Agreement in the House of Lords on November 26, 1985, the Baroness had this to say:

"Being someone who was in Algiers during the trauma of Algerian independence in 1962, I cannot but recognise one or two chilling parallels. For example, to begin with, I remember the running sore that the Algerian conflict was for France as a country. Next, I remember, in the same way as the French settlers felt betrayed by General de Gaulle, who was a French leader they thought they could trust, in the same way, the Unionists feel a keen sense of betrayal — misjudged as I think it is — from a leader and from a government that they believed most sympathetic to their wishes. Nor can I forget the terrible backlash from those enraged French settlers and the havoc they caused after the Evian Agreements of April 1962 and the hatred and the lack of sympathy that those settlers, through their intransigence, brought on themselves from the French of metropolitan France. Finally, I recollect the systematic campaign of provocation that the OAS, the terrorist organisation representing their interests, waged against the Arab community in order to wreck the Evian Agreement. But in the end, as history relates and as your Lordships will remember, the General held firm, and in spite of a terrible sacrifice in human terms the Agreement was honoured."

There are two bona fide parallels in this, the *"running sore"* parallel and the *"sense of betrayal"* parallel. But in what sense can the French settlers' *"terrible backlash"* and the terrorism of the OAS be cited as a parallel with anything that is going on in Northern Ireland? If the Protestants of Northern Ireland are the butt of the *"hatred and lack of sympathy"* of the mainland

British population, this is not because they have been behaving as the French settlers did. It is despite the fact that they have been behaving in an entirely different way, employing the constitutional means at their disposal in an endeavour to have their democratic rights taken into account. In any case, there is no evidence that the mainland British population as a whole is consumed with hatred for the Protestants of Northern Ireland. British intellectuals are merely projecting their own obsessive sentiments onto the public at large when they make assertions of this kind.

Of course, the references to the OAS and so forth, while entirely unjustified by the actual behaviour of the Northern Irish Protestants, have a definite political function. This is to discredit Protestant resistance to the Anglo-Irish Agreement in advance, by smearing it with the guilt-by-association with the OAS. If Protestant gunmen actually were machine-gunning Catholics at bus-stops from speeding cars, systematically assassinating the most innocuous advocates of reconciliation between the two communities, planting plastic explosive all over Belfast and Londonderry and trying repeatedly to kill Mrs. Thatcher, there would be some point in the comparison. But the Protestants are not doing anything of the kind. Barricades, a few burnt cars and the resort to Arthur Scargill's methods (on a much smaller scale than the National Union of Mineworkers) of organising a strike fall a very long way short of what the OAS got up to in Algeria.

Having delivered herself of these unhelpful reminiscences, the Baroness went on to admit that the Algerian episode was not *"a real parallel"* after all. In which case, we are entitled to wonder why she raised the matter in the first place. We are entitled to suspect that this admission was purely for the purpose of covering the Baroness's intellectual flanks, and that the political substance of what she said was contained in the initial suggestion of a real parallel, and a most lurid and emotive parallel at that, rather than in the subsequent formal contradiction of this suggestion.

The Prophet: R.W. Johnson

Bill Johnson is the author of two remarkable books, **How Long will South Africa Survive?** and **The Long March Of The French Left**. They are remarkable in several ways. The book on South Africa presented an uusually hardheaded analysis of the situation, and shocked South African radical émigré circles for its bluntly pessimistic survey of the strategic and tactical options and predelictions of the anti-apartheid and Black nationalist movements. It also contained a fascinating and extraordinarily researched analysis of the politics of the international gold trade. **The Long March Of The French Left** is undoubtedly one of the very best books to have been written on post-war French politics, combining a mastery of French political sociology, an easy familiarity with the French socialist and communist parties, beautifully chosen snap-shots of scenes from French political life and, above all, an all pervading sureness of judgement and touch which endow its conclusions with considerable authority. Moreover, both books are beautifully written, in clear, jargon-free, English, the analysis alternately penetrating, provocative and amusing, but above all lucid and accessible to the lay reader.

In short, Bill Johnson represents much of what is best in Oxford political science, and this is likely to have endowed his journalistic writings with substantial authority in the minds of many of his readers. Which, with regard to the Northern Ireland question, is a very great pity.

The fact that he saw fit to include his 1981 article ("Ireland And The Runcible Men") in the collection of his essays, **The Politics Of Recession**, published by Macmillan in 1985, entitles us to suppose that he stands by what he wrote five years previously. And well he might do so, for he has grounds for thinking now that he got it right then, long before many other pundits. In the most hard-nosed — indeed, cold-blooded — manner, he sketched out very frankly the intellectual rationale for what is now beginning to take place, the British establishment's machiavellian endeavour to expel one and a half million British citizens from the United Kingdom and secure, by degrees, their incorporation against their will in the Irish Republic. He did not only provide the rationale for this endeavour, he foresaw that it would be undertaken. As a professional political scientist, he may be congratulated on his lucidity. He certainly read the British political establishment correctly. But since he uninhibitedly approved of, indeed advocated, the enterprise which he foresaw, he must take his share of the moral responsibility for it. His article gives intellectual respectability to what the British Government is now doing.

Since what the British Government is now doing is dishonest and undemocratic, in short, disreputable in the extreme, it is only right and proper that the most honest and coherent statement of its intellectual rationale to have appeared in print should be subjected to the most searching scrutiny.

Johnson's Format And Premise

After a few preliminary remarks, in which he informs us that all his French friends feel *"both fairly sympathetic to the British dilemma in Ulster and equally convinced that a united Ireland (is) the only right or possible solution,"* having been through the same agony themselves over Algeria,

Johnson presents the substance of his argument in the form of a dialogue with a sceptical Englishman who just cannot get his mind round the Algerian analogy.

This format enables Johnson to set up a string of Aunt Sallies and knock them down again. It is not that the sceptical Englishman is a mere figment of Johnson's imagination, or a caricature. In the thoroughgoing ignorance of the social and political realities of Northern Ireland which Johnson attributes to him, he is undoubtedly representative of his type. Johnson does not need to caricature his Englishman at all, sad to say. He merely needs a typical Englishman, which is to say, a well meaning, sincere but, above all, ignorant Englishman. An Ulster Protestant (as opposed to the standard English intellectual's caricature of an Ulster Protestant) would have made mincemeat of Johnson's analogies. But Johnson chooses not to have a dialogue, even a purely fictional dialogue, with an Ulster Protestant.

Having established, with the help of *le tout Paris*, his premise, namely that the Britishness of Northern Ireland is as much a *"myth"* as was the Frenchness of *l'Algérie française*, and that *"divorce"* from the *"metropolis"* is as inevitable in the case of Ulster as it proved to be in the case of Algeria, Johnson elaborates the alleged parallel point by point. His main thesis is that the Protestant are entirely analogous to the European *"colons"*, can be expected to behave in the same way and should be treated in the same way. If anything, he suggests, they are likely to give less trouble to a decolonising British government than their Algerian counterparts gave de Gaulle.

Before we deal with this premise and this thesis, it is worth while looking at the other points Johnson makes.

Johnson On "Terrorism"

Johnson dismisses the argument that *"we can't give in to terrorism"*, observing that the same argument was heard in France in 1961 and 1962. He does not actually say that we *should* give in to terrorism, but remarks, of those politicians who have taken a tough stand against the terrorists, that *"there are always short-term political gains in doing that"*. The implication is that such politicians (he cites Guy Mollet, Jules Moch and François Mitterand in France and Wilson, Callaghán and Foot) are short-sighted at best, if not miserable self-seeking opportunists.

It is undoubtedly the case that much public denunciation of *"terrorism"* by politicians is humbug. Time and again, governments whose spokesmen have foamed at the mouth in self-righteous indignation a few years earlier have ended up negotiating with the *"terrorists"* and arranging to transfer political power to them. (The architect of Southern Ireland's independence, Michael

Collins, who remains unhonoured to this day by the state he founded, is very much a case in point. In the vocabulary of Whitehall and its Fleet Street poodle, he made the transition from *"gunman"* to *"statesman"* in a matter of weeks.)

But it does not follow from this that governments should invariably *"give in"* to *"terrorists"*. Should Whitehall have given in to the Angry Brigade? Should the Italian Government have given in to the Red Brigades? Should Washington have given in to the demands of the Black Panthers or the Weathermen (whatever those demands were)? Should the West German government have given in to the Baader-Meinhof gang? Should Madrid give in to ETA? Should Paris give in to Corsican separatism? Johnson does not begin to identify the criteria or conditions which may provide political validation for *"giving in"* to *"terrorism"*. Yet these criteria and conditions are not esoteric or even mysterious. They boil down to the question of democratic principle.

The FLN in Algeria could claim to have democratic principles on its side in several fundamental respects. First, the Muslims were the overwhelming majority of the population of French Algeria. Second, the resort to violent means by the FLN occurred only after decades of constitutional political activity. This activity had got the nationalist cause nowhere, but this was not because this cause failed to elicit widespread Muslim support. It was because the Muslims remained disenfranchised for practically the entire colonial period. They were not second-class citizens. They were not citizens at all, but *"natives"* (*indigènes*), subject to a special code (*le code de l'indigénat*). They were subjects. And when, finally, they were allowed to vote in elections to an Algerian assembly in 1948, these elections were massively rigged by the colonial authorities. Many nationalist candidates who managed nonetheless to get elected in 1948 were promptly arrested thereafter on trumped-up charges. There simply was no constitutional means open to Algerian nationalism to translate whatever majority support it might acquire in Algeria into political power. By 1958, when de Gaulle returned to power in France, the FLN would probably have won a free election in Algeria and by 1961, when the serious negotiations began, it certainly would have done so. De Gaulle's decision to negotiate with the *"terrorists"* could accordingly claim substantial democratic legitimacy on that account.

None of this applies to the *"terrorists"* in Northern Ireland. The Provisional IRA has employed violence not because peaceful, constitutional avenues are closed to the Catholic nationalist cause, but because this cause enjoys only minority support in Northern Ireland, and cannot therefore ever hope to win by democratic means. The Muslims were 90 per cent of the population of French Algeria. The Catholics are little more than a third of the population of Northern Ireland. And it is quite wrong to suppose that the entire Catholic community in Northern Ireland wants a United Ireland. Repeated opinion surveys have shown that between 40 and 50 per cent of the Catholic community actively prefer to retain British citizenship, and that Direct Rule from Westminster has enjoyed the approval of as much as 80 per cent of the Catholic community. (It is remarkable how systematically British politicians and the media have overlooked the solid evidence repeatedly produced by these surveys. It is difficult to believe that this has not been deliberate. See Appendix.)

In short, in palpable contrast to the Algerian affair, there is no democratic justification whatever for *"giving in"* to *"terrorism"* in Northern Ireland, that is, for conceding the IRA's demand for a United Ireland.

Irish Nationalism's Double Act, Or The Uses Of Humbug

It should be noted that there is absolutely no difference of substance or principle between conceding a United Ireland — or a stepping-stone to a United Ireland — to John Hume's SDLP and Garret FitzGerald's Coalition Government or conceding it to the IRA outright. The difference is purely a matter of form. Nobody would be so much as dreaming of a United Ireland if the IRA had not been busy softening up the British political establishment for the last sixteen years, and nobody knows this better than John Hume and Garret FitzGerald. Their function is to provide the acceptable face of nationalism to which the concession can decently be made. But the acceptable face of nationalism would be of no account whatsoever were it not for the purposeful, intelligent and relentless activity of the unacceptable face of nationalism. Unconstitutional nationalism keeps *"constitutional"* nationalism in business. And whenever the IRA has begun to find the going just a little too hard, Hume and FitzGerald and the rest of the *"constitutional"* nationalists, from Dick Spring to Archbishop O'Fiaich, have been quick to step in with well disguised but nonetheless effective moral support: putting pressure on the British government over the IRA hunger strikers, for instance. Did Hume or FitzGerald ever give moral support to those Catholics who had joined the Ulster Defence Regiment and who thus held out the prospect of establishing it as a non-sectarian military force? Not at all. They said and did nothing while the IRA was systematically assassinating such Catholics. And Dublin has used every hypocritical pretext in the book to explain away its *"inability"* to extradite wanted terrorists to the North. The amazing thing is not that Hume and FitzGerald should have behaved in this way, but that the British government and media should have persistently allowed them to get away with it.

Whenever FitzGerald and Hume denounce the IRA, this is the most consummate humbug, but it is politically necessary humbug and the IRA understands this political necessity and does not get upset about it. War heroes and cabinet ministers in the Republic are not blown to kingdom come. The notion that the IRA is as much a threat to the Republic as it is to the United Kingdom is without foundation. It is simply part of the humbug which is Dublin's principal contribution to the national cause.

But when the British government gives every appearance of accepting the humbug of FitzGerald and Hume at face value, this is also humbug on its part. But it is neither politically necessary nor in the British national interest, unless this national interest is defined as requiring the expulsion of one and a half million British citizens from the United Kingdom, a proposition which has never been put to the British electorate, with good reason. The Jesuits of Dublin and Derry can (perhaps) sincerely and genuinely justify their humbug to themselves in so far as it serves a transcendental national ideal. But the humbug of Whitehall is merely cynical, if not treasonous.

Whose Consent Is It Anyway?

It is arguably to Johnson's credit that he does not for one moment pretend that giving in to the *"terrorists"* has anything to do with democratic principle. When his sceptical but also naive Englishman protests that *"we've said over and over again that we won't do anything without the consent of the people of Ulster... we can't go back on our promises,"* Johnson replies, with brutal candour, *"The truthful answer to this is: yes we can; and no, the consent of the Ulster Protestants doesn't really matter"*. He rationalises this encouragement to renege upon the principle of consent by remarking that *"it is a question of whose consent, after all"*, an observation he elaborates as follows:

> *"The French could have conceded Algerian independence but kept the most developed part, Algiers, which was predominantly French, for themselves. They could then have held referenda galore in Algiers, with repeated massive votes for continuing integration with France. It wouldn't have solved anything. The Algerians would have remained second-class citizens in Algiers, and they would never have tolerated the situation.*
>
> *"Effectively, that's just what the British have done in Ireland — drawn a line around the most developed part which was predominantly Protestant and kept Catholics there in a state of second-class citizenship. If you wanted to hold a meaningful referendum over Algerian independence you*

had to ask all the people of Algeria or (less clearly) all the people of France what they wanted. If you want a meaningful referendum over Irish reunification, you have to ask all the people of Ireland or (less clearly) all the people of Britain."

The first paragraph in this passage is indisputable. The second paragraph puts forward an absurd principle, which it is crucially unable to formulate clearly, and which it supports with a breathtaking misrepresentation of Northern Ireland's history. This misrepresentation will be dealt with in due course. Let us first consider the principle. To do this, we need to improve upon Johnson's self-confessedly unclear statement of it. This statement admits of only three possible interpretations.

1. In a conflict involving a colonial power and a colony, and concerning the political future of this colony, the issue is to be decided by a referendum in the metropolis alone (e.g., asking all the people of France what they want). This is indefensible. It concedes in advance the right of the metropolis to determine the political future of the colony, which is, presumably, precisely the point at issue.

2. The issue is decided by a referendum in the metropolis and the colony simultaneously. De Gaulle may have managed to get away with this in the Algerian case, because circumstances enabled him to do so, but as a principle it too is indefensible. The population of the metropolis may be either larger than that of the colony (as was true of France in relation to Algeria) or very much smaller (e.g., the United Kingdom and India). Thus the prospects of the population of the colony being able to exercise the right of self-determination may come, in practice, to depend essentially on whether or not its population is numerically larger than that of its colonial oppressor. By this principle, the United Kingdom could have effortlessly outvoted the supporters of separatist nationalism in Kenya, Ghana, every British colonial possession in the Pacific and, for that matter, of course, Ireland. The notion is self-evidently absurd.

3. The issue is decided by a referendum of the population of the colony alone. This is the only principle which is defensible on democratic grounds. And although de Gaulle held referenda in France, because he was a prudent man and deemed it necessary to cover his rear by doing so, this was the principle which was actually operative in the Algerian case. The French electorate had learned to think realistically about Algeria by 1961 and 1962, and effectively contented itself with ratifying the democratic balance of forces in Algeria.

But while this is without question the only defensible principle, it is not enough merely to proclaim it. It is necessary to make it operative in a given case. An academic political philosopher, free to spend his days in the contemplation of eternal verities, may content himself with enunciating and justifying the principle, and not bother himself with the awkward and tiresome business whereby the word becomes flesh. But a practical politician must concern himself with this business. And any British politician with an iota of competence and historical awareness will know that colonies are apt to come in all shapes and sizes and are even more apt to contain anything but tidily homogeneous native populations. It may well be the case that a given colony contains not one coherent native population, but several, which are clearly differentiated by national culture and national interest. It may also be the case that one of these populations enjoys a clear numerical preponderance. Does it follow from the abstract principle enunciated above that this majority population has *carte blanche* to override the interests and wishes of the others? Did the Hindu majority in India have the right to keep the Muslim minority in an all-Indian state against its will? British rule unified India. The unity of India was a function of the British presence, and this unity was that of an administrative unit rather than a political community. The imperialist nostalgia which has recently been so rampant on British television and cinema screens may lead us to regret that India's unity did not survive the Raj. But can anyone seriously suggest that the democratic principle of self-determination would have been more fully realised by Hindu nationalist suppression of Muslim separatism than it was by Partition and the subsequent emergence of the sovereign states of Pakistan and, for that matter, Bangladesh?

It is remarkable that, in his search for analogies, Johnson should have embarked so readily for Algeria and should have entirely ignored the other great instance of partition in the history of British decolonisation.

In speaking of Irish *"reunification"* in the passage quoted above, Johnson reveals his ignorance along with his bias. The suggestion that Ireland was a political unit prior to British rule is simply untrue. It is an untruth which is assiduously put about by Irish nationalists, but anyone with as much as a nodding acquaintance with Irish history will know that it is not to be taken seriously. (And one suspects that Johnson himself would be the last person to take the pretensions of nationalist historiography seriously when encountered in other contexts. Algeria north of the Sahara was administratively unified by Turkish rule between 1516 and 1830. The present-day boundaries of Algeria, incorporating the Saharan region, are a legacy of French colonialism. In so far as one can speak of a unified Algerian nation, it is a product of Turkish and French rule. The indigenous Arab and Berber tribes of what is now Algeria were quite incapable of establishing a unified Algerian state of their own accord. They did not have it in them to do so. They were remaining entirely true to their own nature in neglecting to do so. The rulers of independent Algeria are disposed to project the existence of what is, in fact, a very young nation back into the distant past. It is politically expedient for them to do this. But it has no foundation in historical fact. And so it is with Ireland.)

Ireland was unified by British rule. And when the time came for the British to abandon their rule over Ireland, they found, to their surprise, that Ireland contained not one coherent national community, but two. The processes of economic, cultural and political development which had occurred in Ireland during the centuries of British rule had given rise to a Catholic community, which was vigorously seeking to go its own way and set up a sovereign Catholic state for a Catholic people, and a smaller but, if anything, more coherent, Protestant community in the north-east which was determined not to become an oppressed minority in a Catholic state. The Partition of Ireland was a democratic solution to the problem inherent in this state of affairs. The Protestants of Ulster had as much right as the Muslims of India to determine their own political future. If the Catholic Irish minority in the United Kingdom had the right to opt out of the United Kingdom, the Protestant Irish minority in Ireland had an equal right to opt out of what was unquestionably going to be a zealously and intolerantly Catholic state. Those who invoke the right of self-determination for themselves should beware of seeking to deny it to others. And the right of self-determination, while it unequivocally includes the right to establish a sovereign state, does not oblige those who would exercise it to exercise it in this way. They may equally choose some other arrangement, such as autonomy within a larger political whole. Or they may choose to remain where they are.

So much for how the third, democratic principle should have been applied in 1920-21. The way things actually worked out at that time was consistent with how the principle which Johnson invokes should have been applied. The Partition of Ireland was consistent with this principle. If it did not provide a full and lasting solution to the national question in Ireland, this is not because Partition itself was wrong or mistaken. It is because there was no way in which Partition could avoid leaving national minorities on both sides of the border, and because, whereas the Protestant minority in the South resigned itself to its fate and attempted to make the best of life in the Republic, the Catholic minority in the North never did either of these things. To say this is not to reproach the Catholic minority in the North. It was a much larger proportion of the total population of the North than the Protestant minority in the South was of the total population of the Republic. This in itself need not have mattered. But it was encouraged by successive governments of the Republic and the 1937 Constitution to resist its fate and to maintain itself in irredentist disaffection from the United Kingdom. And by imposing devolved government on the province and by establishing a total boycott of the province by the mainland political parties, the British political establishment made it impossible for the Catholic minority in Northern Ireland to participate in the political life of the United Kingdom on the same basis as everyone else and thus condemned it to remain entrenched in the attitude of irredentist disaffection. And having thus sabotaged the prospect of Partition providing an effective solution to the national question, the British political establishment has had the effrontery to blame Catholic disaffection in Northern Ireland entirely upon the Protestant community there.

But we are not now in 1920-1. We are in 1986. The situation in Northern Ireland ceased to be analogous with Algeria in 1962 or India in 1947 no less than 65 years ago. The situation is analogous rather to that of Alsace-Lorraine. Two states, which are close neighbours and have ancient and complicated ties of interdependence, exchange, and antagonism are in dispute over a clearly defined territory. To suggest, as Johnson does, that the question should be resolved today by means of a referendum of the population of the island of Ireland is analogous to suggesting that the future of Alsace-Lorraine should have been decided by a referendum of the population of Alsace-Lorraine plus Germany. The majority of the inhabitants of Alsace-Lorraine were German-speaking. Germany's irredentist claim to Alsace-Lorraine had a great deal of history (800 years of the Holy Roman Empire, for a start) on its side, and the geographical argument did not count against it. But it just so happened that the majority of the population of Alsace-Lorraine did not want to be incorporated into the German state. As Karl Marx observed in 1871, *"the Germans dare not pretend that the people of Alsace-Lorraine pant for the German embrace"**. Partly because the inhabitants of Alsace-Lorraine were Catholics, but also for other reasons, they actively preferred citizenship of the French Republic. And eventually, after three wars and countless loss of life, the principle that the people of Alsace-Lorraine should be allowed to choose for themselves which state to belong to was realised in practice.

By speaking as if the situation in Northern Ireland today is analogous to that of Algeria in 1962, Johnson is engaging in wishful thinking. He is indulging his regret that Partition occurred. He is wishing away, and dismissing as of no account, 65 years of history. He is assuming that the event of Partition was that extremely rare thing, an event which occurs in the absence of sufficient cause. He is echoing the combination of nostalgia, voluntarism, bad history and contempt for the rights of the living which is fundamental to the worldview of contemporary Republican irredentism.

---

*Karl Marx: **The Civil War In France** (in Marx and Engels: **Selected Works In One Volume**, Lawrence and Wishart, London, 1968, pp. 252-313), page 268.

Consent And The South

Johnson's claim that the population of the South should be party to any referendum on the future of Northern Ireland, while indefensible, would at least be understandable were it based on the belief that this population cares deeply about what happens north of the border and is all for Irish unity. But it is not based on that belief.

On the contrary, Johnson cites the case of Dr. Conor Cruise O'Brien, and his discovery *"that his colleagues in the Irish government privately did not want Irish unity"* and appears to accept the content of this *"discovery"*. This realism in no way deters Johnson from remarking that

*"in the end it doesn't matter what the Irish government — Haughey or FitzGerald — privately want. Publicly, they, their voters, and their constitution demand a united Ireland. This is very fortunate for Britain — we would have a far greater problem if Dublin could say publicly that it doesn't want Ulster at any price. Happily, this is a political impossibility: we can drop Ulster in Dublin's lap any time we want. We may be handing them a bloody and costly horror, but they'll have to **sound** pleased."*

So the analogy with Algeria cited earlier is now completely forgotten. While the Algerians would not have stood for partition, the Irish are not going to be able to avoid having a United Ireland thrust upon them, however much they might like to do so.

Johnson is unquestionably right in his estimation of the private wishes of the Irish political establishment in general. (The particular case of Garret FitzGerald is a partial exception. FitzGerald is a politician who appears genuinely to believe whatever it is that he happens to be saying at any given moment. Some years ago, he was publicly saying that Southern Ireland was an oppressively priest-ridden state and that he could entirely understand why no self-respecting Protestant would want to have anything to do with the place. Shortly afterwards, he facilitated Catholic social doctrine on abortion being entrenched with unprecedented force in the Republic's Constitution.) There is no doubt that the resort to irredentist tub-thumping on the North has been largely, if not entirely, for internal party political purposes down South. This would not have mattered if the British government had not, for reasons of its own, decided to take this tub-thumping at face value. The Irish government is, as Johnson clearly sees, about to be hoist with its own petard.

But it is not only a question of the Irish political establishment. The Southern Irish public in general is similarly ambivalent about Irish Unity. There is no doubt that a general sentimental predisposition in favour of a United Ireland is widespread in the South, along with a long-standing incomprehension of the Protestant community in Northern Ireland. But this general sentimental predisposition is only one among several general sentimental predispositions which may be observed to be widespread in Southern Ireland. It would be entirely wrong to attach any particular political significance to it. It is not an issue which mobilises the Southern Irish electorate. In recent times, general elections in the Republic have usually been lost by the party which sought to make its stand on the North a major plank of its platform. It is hard to believe that Johnson, a professional political scientist, is unaware of this significant little fact.

Thus Johnson's talk of a referendum throughout the island of Ireland is a red-herring, designed to distract his readers' attention from the fact that he is, in reality, proposing that the principle of unification by consent be abandoned. Whether the North wants to join the Republic or not, whether the Republic really wants it or not, *"we can drop Ulster in Dublin's lap any time we want."*

Bad History

"The French could have conceded Algerian independence but kept the most developed part, Algiers, which was predominantly French, for themselves... Effectively, that's just what the British have done in Ireland — drawn a line around the most developed part which was predominantly Protestant and kept Catholics there in a state of second-class citizenship."

This is a misrepresentation of how the Partition of Ireland occurred. But it is also a flawed analogy in its own terms.

Algiers was the capital of Turkish Algeria from 1516 to 1830. From 1830 onwards, it was the administrative and business capital of French Algeria, the main port and the centre of the country's road and rail network, as well as its educational system. It was the country's natural and obvious capital. Johnson is evidently right in his assessment of what the Algerian nationalist reaction would have been should the French have attempted to retain Algiers. But it is really rather pointless to suggest that the French could have retained Algiers. The idea was self-evidently not on. Nobody ever seriously suggested it, not even the OAS.

The Irish counterpart to Algiers was not Belfast, but Dublin. The Algerian counterpart to Belfast, if there was one at all, was Oran. The idea of creating a European redoubt in the Oran region was actually mooted in late 1962. French intelligence was aware that the OAS was considering this, and de Gaulle issued orders to his General Officer Commanding, Oran, General Joseph Katz, to use all the force at his disposal to put down any such attempt if necessary. In the event, no such attempt was made. The fact that the idea of a European redoubt in the Oran region was mooted so late in the day (and mooted not by any local representative of the European population but by the OAS Chief for Oran, Paul Gardy, former Inspector-General of the Foreign Legion) and that the attempt to put it into practice was never made, strongly suggests that it was an extremely far-fetched idea.

Algeria was not partitioned because the conditions for partitioning Algeria did not exist. But the partition of Ireland cannot be said to have been a far-fetched idea. Ireland was partitioned.

Johnson states that what the French *"could have"* done (i.e., what, as a matter of mere empirical fact, they proved incapable of doing) in Algeria is *"just what the British have done in Ireland...etc."* I have described this statement as a misrepresentation of how Partition actually occurred. But there is a sense in which it is not a misrepresentation, but a broadly accurate statement. It all depends on what is being designated by the term, *"the British"*.

If the term is used to designate not only the people of Great Britain (England, Wales and Scotland) but also the people of Northern Ireland, or at any rate, that element of the Northern Ireland population which regards itself as British, then Johnson's statement becomes formally true, on condition that it is understood that it is the actions of only a part of the British population, the Northern Ireland part, which are being credited with having brought Partition about. And it is surely implicit in Johnson's view of the Protestants as *"colons"* that they are indeed to be regarded as British. If they are not British, how can they be *"colons"*? But Johnson appears not to be entirely consistent in his view of the Protestants as *"colons"*, *ergo* British. Although he clearly thinks they should be treated as *"colons"* and may end up behaving like their counterparts in Algeria in opposing a Gaullist solution to the Northern Ireland problem, he appears not to expect them to emulate their Algerian counterparts in returning *en masse* to the metropolis. It is surely implicit in his admission that *"we may be handing them a bloody and costly horror"* when we *"drop Ulster in Dublin's lap"* that he expects the Protestants to stay where they are. They will merely become Dublin's problem, and no longer ours. All of which strongly suggests that the Protestants are not quite British, not in the sense of being part of Johnson's *"we"*. Elsewhere in **The Politics Of Recession**, Johnson uses the terms *"Britain"* and *"England"* interchangeably. His otherwise irreproachable essay on the Falklands war, **My Country Right Or Left?**, for example, begins with the sentence: *"England is at war again"* — an assessment of the situation to which the obvious reply is: tell that to the war widows of Glamorgan.

It does not make sense in terms of Johnson's overall argument to assume that he is using the term *"the British"* to include the Protestants of Northern Ireland in the passage quoted dealing with the origin of Partition. He is undoubtedly using it to designate the English, or at most the inhabitants of Great Britain (England, Wales and Scotland) alone. It is clearly his view that the mainland British, and the British government in particular, were the artisans of Partition. Even were he to include the Protestants of Northern Ireland within the category of *"the British"*, he is clearly unable to concede that they were the primary artisans of Partition, for to do so would be to admit that they had been capable of precisely the response to their predicament of which the *"colons"* in Algeria proved entirely incapable, and that they therefore differ from these *"colons"* in a most significant way.

Therefore Johnson attributes primary, if not total, responsibility for Partition to the mainland British and their government. He echoes, once more, the standard Republican view. And he comprehensively misrepresents what occurred.

It is axiomatic for Irish Republicanism that the Partition of Ireland was a contrivance of British imperialism, and that British imperialism was motivated by self-interest, and that this self-interest was primarily economic in nature. It was prepared to let the under-developed four-fifths of Ireland go their own way, but determined to hang on to the developed bit in the northeast. Is this not precisely what Johnson is saying?

The problem with this interpretation of the politics of Partition is that it leaves out of account the actual policy of successive British governments during the period in question. Gladstone's policy was to concede the whole of Ireland to Irish nationalism under Home Rule. This was also Asquith's policy, in the third Home Rule Bill of 1912. And there can be no doubt that had Asquith's successor as leader of the Liberal Party, David Lloyd George, been able to concede the whole 32 counties to Michael Collins and Arthur Griffith in 1921 he would have done so. In the event he did his best. He could not deliver up the North to the nationalists, but he could refuse to allow it to be reintegrated into the political life of the rest of the United Kingdom by imposing a devolved government upon it and thereby keeping it at arm's length from Great Britain. And he agreed with Collins and Griffith that a Council of Ireland would be set up to which the newly created Northern Ireland Government would be obliged to send delegates. Lloyd George did everything in his power to hold open the prospect of an eventual unification of Ireland under nationalist rule. That was the policy of the British government at the time that Partition occurred. It was entirely in keeping with the spirit and intention of Asquith's policy and that of Gladstone before him.

The plain fact of the matter is that, far from seeking to keep Northern Ireland in the United Kingdom, successive British governments in the hey-day of British imperialism tried extremely hard to get rid of the place. They did not see Northern Ireland as an indispensable asset, they saw it as an awkward encumbrance, much as it is seen today. They did not impose Partition on Ireland, Partition was imposed on the British government by Protestant Ulster. It is essential to Irish Republican irredentism to deny this fact. And it is essential to an adequate conception of the contemporary Northern Ireland question to recognise it, and to weigh its implications.

A Matter Of Geography

Although Johnson agrees with the Republican conception of Northern Ireland history in at least certain important respects, it would be quite wrong to suggest that his overall argument is Republican in spirit or flavour. To suggest this would be self-evidently inconsistent with my earlier claim that Johnson's view of the matter is both hard-nosed and frank. Not for one moment does he buy any of the clap-trap about the alleged 'socialist' character of the IRA and Provisional Sinn Fein upon which the 'solidarity' of the mainland British Left is so laughably predicated. Nor does he have any illusions about the social character of the Irish Republic. Indeed, he urges his progressive English readers, who may be assumed to have illusions about the IRA, to

"note that the IRA will be just as insignificant within a united green fairly reactionary Ireland as the FLN militants turned out to be within orthodox Muslim Algeria"

The salient aspect of this passage is not what it says about the IRA or the FLN or the putative analogy between them, but what it says about the Irish Republic. Johnson is well aware that to come under the Republic is to come under the hegemony of the Roman Catholic Church. He does not draw the obvious conclusion from this, that the Ulster Unionists have always been dead right about the South, and have had ample grounds for resisting incorporation in the South, but it is clearly implicit in Johnson's illusion-free view of the South.

But, while saying these things — and they are things that no spokesman for Republican irredentism could ever say, at any rate in public — Johnson does not allow that they justify the Unionist point of view. He manages to evade the awkward implications of his own illusion-free view of the South by invoking what he clearly imagines to be an all-powerful counter-argument, which he introduces and endeavours to reinforce with the Algerian analogy once again:

> *"In Algeria, the **colons** were even more aghast at the prospect of becoming citizens of a backward state, where they would be subject to the anti-feminist and obsolete morality of Muslim law. In the end, however, the fact was that Algeria was part of the Muslim world; staying there would mean bowing the knee to the hegemony of Islam. For the few **colons** who stayed it didn't turn out as bad as they feared; but that wasn't the point: they just had to choose what mattered to them most.*
>
> *"Being part of Ireland **means** being part of a predominantly Roman Catholic country. It's a matter of geography, not religion."*

There is a Republican song by Dominic Behan called **Thank God We're Surrounded By Water**. Once again, *in extremis*, Johnson, who is so profoundly un-Republican in spirit, calls upon Republican dogma to get him out of an awkward corner into which his own lack of illusions has led him.

Algeria was not only part of the Muslim world. The same could be said for much of the Balkans, after all. Algeria was and is part of Africa. The journey from metropolitan France to transmediterranean France was a journey from one continent to another. And the actual physical distance was very considerable. Only a narrow strip of water separates Europe from Africa at the southernmost tip of Spain. But from Marseille to Algiers is 402 nautical miles. Even today, with the most modern ships, the voyage takes a minimum of 25 hours and frequently more, as the present writer knows from repeated experience. The French expeditionary force which captured Algiers in 1830 took six days to cross the Mediterranean.

Ireland and mainland Britain are not in different continents. They are part of the same, north-western, region of Europe and within this, of the same geographical ensemble known as the British Isles. The strip of sea known as the North Channel which separates Northern Ireland from that part of the British mainland known as Scotland is little more than 20 miles across. At its narrowest point, between Fair Head in County Antrim and the Mull of Kintyre, it is a mere 12½ miles across. This is much less than the distance which separates the Isle of Lewis from the Scottish mainland (24 miles); it is even less than the distance between the Isle of Harris and the Isle of Skye (16¾ miles). But it would not make a jot of difference if it were more.

The implication of Johnson's argument is that islands are natural political units and that even the narrowest strips of sea are natural political frontiers. This is a principle which would create havoc if it were applied wherever geographical circumstances suggested that it could be applied. It would make nonsense of the states of Malaysia, Indonesia and the Philippines for a start, not to mention Greece. And is not Africa surrounded by water? Should not the Africans be informed that geography demands that they realise forthwith the pan-African destiny which the more far-sighted of their leaders have so often invoked? And if this principle holds good for islands, why should it not also apply to peninsulas? Are these not also geographical units? Should not Portugal abandon its pretensions to independent statehood and accept that geography dictates its *"reunification"* into an all-Iberian republic under Spanish hegemony? Here, truly, one can say that *"it's a matter of geography, not religion"*. They are all Roman Catholics, after all.

It might be objected that I have answered Johnson's argument by resorting to the dubious device of *reductio ad absurdum*. This objection is groundless. Johnson's argument is absurd to begin with. To say this is not to heap any particular opprobrium upon him. It would be extremely unfair to single Johnson out in this matter. The absurd argument from geography has become one of the most regular refrains in the repertoire of the choir of British and Irish opponents of the Union. In no way can Bill Johnson be held responsible for originating this argument.

Moreover, it is an argument which he has been quick to reject in other contexts. In his brilliant discussion of the Falklands war, he pours justifiable scorn on those elements of British Left and liberal opinion who cited the distance between the United Kingdom and the Falklands as grounds for opposing the dispatch of the British Task Force, noting with irony that this view amounted to taking *"geography as the queen of the moral sciences again"*.

It is in no small measure because British intellectuals and politicians have repeatedly applied to Northern Ireland principles which they know to be unsound and which they would not dream of applying elsewhere that the Northern Ireland problem is still with us, and still killing people.

Catholicism, Islam And Tolerance

The analogy which Johnson invokes between Roman Catholicism in Ireland and Islam in Algeria is extremely apt in several ways. There can be no doubt that the ideological core of anti-British nationalism in Ireland was furnished by Roman Catholicism, and the role of Islam in the Algerian nationalist movement, while qualified by the presence of important secular tendencies, was of fundamental significance and not in dispute. So much is common ground. And had we the leisure to explore this common ground further, there is no doubt that a number of additional parallels in matters of detail would be discovered.

But there are several respects in which Roman Catholicism in Ireland and Islam in Algeria maybe said to differ significantly. These differences are pertinent to the overall point at issue, in so far as they have a bearing upon the comparative position of non-Catholics in the Irish Republic and non-Muslims in independent Algeria. The two most important differences are these. First, Roman Catholicism has traditionally been intolerant of Protestantism, whereas Islam has traditionally been tolerant of both the Christian and the Jewish faiths. Second, Roman Catholicism is not only a faith, it is a church; more than any other version of Christianity, it is characterised by an elaborate and strictly disciplined hierarchy and, unlike any other version of Christianity, this hierarchy is international in character, with a clear apex in the papacy. There is no church or clergy or hierarchy, or counterpart of Vatican or Pope, in Islam, least of all in the majority Sunni variant of Islam which prevails in North Africa. Let us examine these two points of difference more fully.

The difference between Roman Catholicism and Protestantism is a difference within the common religion of Christianity, whereas the difference between Islam and Christianity is a difference between distinct religions based upon, and validated by, separate bodies of holy scripture. It may be suggested that this is an abstract classificatory distinction without political significance. But to suggest this is to overlook the fact that variants of the same religion are frequently more intolerant of one another than they are of entirely distinct religions, because these variants are competing for the same social and cultural terrain. (The same is true, of course, of variants of certain developed secular ideologies, of which the most notorious example is Marxist-Leninism.)

Islam has traditionally been tolerant of both Christianity and Judaism. (The national division in colonial Algeria was not simply a Christian-Muslim division. There was a significant and long-established Jewish community as well. This was assimilated into the French communty following the Cremieux decree of 1870.) The Islamic states of the pre-modern period discriminated between the Muslim and non-Muslim elements of their populations and accorded a privileged position to the former. They cannot seriously be criticised on that account; their European contemporaries also discriminated between the various elements of their populations, the vast mass of which were disenfranchised subjects, not free citizens. The important point is that these Islamic states, while practising this religious discrimination, nonetheless recognised both their Jewish and their Christian subjects as *"people of the book"* (*ahl el kitab*) and respected their right to practise their religions without interference. They were free to convert to Islam if they wished, but they were under no particular pressure to do so and were not the object of persecution for their beliefs.

Roman Catholicism most certainly cannot claim a comparable tradition of tolerance with regard to Protestantism. To say this is not to condemn Roman Catholicism. It would have been entirely unreasonable to expect Roman Catholicism to behave towards the Protestant faith with the same easy-going tolerance which Islam displayed towards Christianity and Judaism. To tolerate difference is one thing; to tolerate error is another. And, from the point of view of Roman Catholicism, Protestantism was not merely error, it was heresy.

The historical relationship between Islam and both Christianity and Judaism is crucially different from that between Catholicism and Protestantism. Judaism and Christianity preceded Islam. They were firmly established religions long before Islam emerged, and Islam emerged in the first instance as a local variant on the established tradition of scripturalist monotheism which Judaism and Christianity already embodied. Islam was a self-conscious product of this tradition and, while it considered itself to be the definitive expression of this tradition (regarding Mohammed as the *"seal of prophecy"*, i.e., the last of the prophets, God's messengers) and, in particular, more rigorously monotheistic than Christianity, it was bound to feel considerable respect for its precursors and has, historically, done so.

The relationship between Catholicism and Protestantism is the exact opposite of this. Catholicism was the established embodiment of the Christian faith when Protestantism developed. And Protestantism developed, not as a later and more complete version of the Christian message, nourishing sentiments of filial piety towards its Catholic precursor, but as a fundamentalist revolt against Catholicism which it stigmatised as a decadent perversion of that message. It is therefore not to be wondered at that Protestantism should have been in turn denounced as heresy by the Catholic Church, and that the instinctive reflex of this church towards this heresy should have been to extirpate it wherever possible.

The intolerance which Catholicism has historically demonstrated for Protestantism has had its counterparts in the history of Islam. The most notable instance concerns the doctrines of what was known as the Mu'tazila school. Mu'tazilism was a kind of extreme rationalist development within Islam which evoked support among both Sunni and Shi'a Muslims. It was particularly opposed to anthropomorphic conceptions of God and vigorously attacked the doctrine of predestination, arguing that men were fully responsible for their own acts. There are certain parallels with aspects of Protestant Christianity, although these should not be overstated and the differences should not be overlooked. But for our present purpose this is neither here nor there. The point is that the Mu'tazila school came to be regarded as intolerable by the custodians of Islamic orthodoxy. It was accordingly denounced as blasphemous and comprehensively suppressed.

Thus Islam too has had its heresies and has been intolerant of them. It is no part of the argument which is being stated here to suggest that Roman Catholicism is, in general, more intolerant than Islam. The point is merely that Islam has historically been tolerant of Christianity and Judaism, but Catholicism has been intolerant of Protestantism.

A Christian or a Jewish Frenchman in colonial Algeria could hardly view the prospect of being incorporated into a sovereign Muslim state with enthusiasm. But he would have had no valid reason to expect to be the object of religious persecution in such a state. But an Ulster Protestant would have needed to be a confirmed optimist in order to expect his religious beliefs and their practical expression to be the object of an easy-going tolerance on the part of the militantly Catholic state which was in prospect in Southern Ireland. History afforded him no examples of Catholic tolerance of the Protestant heresy where Catholicism had the power to indulge its intolerance.

(It may be pointed out that Protestantism has also, on occasion, been guilty of intolerance with regard to Catholicism and notably so in Ireland, where Catholics were for long subject to what were known as the *"penal laws"*. But to make this point is to misunderstand the argument which is being stated here. It is no part of this argument to moralise about the phenomenon of religious intolerance, let alone to award marks for good or bad behaviour to the various religions or denominations in question. The function of this argument is not to referee a moral boxing match and declare one of the contenders to be the winner on points. It is to bring to the reader's attention a politically significant difference between the Irish and the Algerian cases with respect to the religious issue. Moreover, the penalisation of Catholicism in Ireland was motivated by political, not religious, considerations. Its purpose was not to stamp out the Catholic faith, but to emasculate its political influence, an influence which had been repeatedly put at the service of feudal/Royalist counter-revolution in Britain since the middle of the 16th century. It is entirely misleading to portray this as an instance of religious persecution properly so-called. It had nothing of the spirit of the Inquisition about it. Moreover, the penal laws in Ireland were much less severe than the anti-Catholic laws adopted during the French Revolution, and the last of them were abolished in 1793 and 1829.)

Church And State

Catholicism constituted the ideological core of anti-British nationalism in Ireland. But it did far more than that. Through its Church, it provided constant leadership of nationalist public opinion. The Catholic hierarchy did not attempt to monopolise the functions of political leadership, let alone perform the functions of military leadership when the national conflict with the British entered its military phase. But the hierarchy retained effective control over the political allegiances of the Catholic population, and in virtue of this influence engaged in general supervision of the specifically political wing of the nationalist movement. It was the hierarchy which secured the fall of the Protestant, Parnell, from the leadership of the movement for Irish Home Rule. And, in 1918, it was the hierarchy which secured the triumph of Sinn Fein at the polls at the expense of John Redmond's Irish Parliamentary Party. (The IPP had previously been the beneficiary of the hierarchy's support, but lost this between 1916 and 1918, essentially because Sinn Fein had a more intransigeant position on the North.)

Since the constitution of the independent Irish state in 1921, the Catholic Church has continued to exercise a general hegemony over the society and a quite specific and detailed supervision over successive governments. In matters, not only of faith, but morals in general, and thus social and cultural policy as a whole, its views are explicitly translated into, and faithfully reflected by, government policy.

The relationship of the Catholic Church to the state in Southern Ireland has no parallel in other Catholic countries. The power of the hierarchy over the government is a consequence of its general hegemony over the society. While the relationship between the Church and its flock is unequivocally authoritarian in Ireland, there is nothing irksome in this authoritarianism as it is experienced by Irish Catholics. The Catholic Church in Ireland is without question the most genuinely popular Catholic Church in the world. It is the heart and backbone of the Irish nation, and its hegemony is accepted with enthusiasm. And this hegemony is that of a Church which is guided by and purveys a comprehensive doctrine known as Ultramontanism, one of the cardinal tenets of which is unquestioning obedience to the Pope, whose infallibility it proclaims.

Algeria differs from Ireland in every one of these respects.

Of course Algeria is a Muslim country. The Constitution enshrines the role of Islam as the state religion and the head of state must be a Muslim. This official status of Islam, first established in the Constitution of 1963, was confirmed in the National Charter adopted by referendum in 1976 and in the 1976 Constitution, and has recently been given even greater emphasis in the revised National Charter adopted this year. And there are many respects in which government policy is inspired by Islamic precepts.

Thus the Islamic religion undoubtedly plays an important part in the affairs of state in independent Algeria. But it is important not to exaggerate or misconceive the significance of this. Algeria, unlike Iran, does not describe itself as an Islamic Republic, for the very good reason that it is not one. It is not a religious state, even if it cannot properly be described as a secular state either. As Marx pointed out

"the truly religious state is the theocratic state; the prince of such states must be either the God of religion, Jehovah himself, as in the Jewish state, God's representative, the Dalai Lama, as in Tibet, or finally... they must all submit to a church which is an 'infallible church'. For if, as in Protestantism, there is no supreme head of the church, the domination of religion is nothing but the religion of domination, the cult of the will of the government."*

There is no church in Algeria, still less an *"infallible"* one with a supreme head. Sunni Islam, to which over 99 per cent of Algerian Muslims adhere, has no clergy whatever. It has an entirely egalitarian conception of the *"community of the faithful"* (*umma*). The religious leaders of the community are not priests (let alone father-confessors), but doctors of law (*'alim*, plural *'ulama*), whose authority is not conferred on them by appointment from above, but derives from their possession of knowledge (*'ilm*) of law and

---

*Karl Marx: **The Leading Article Of No. 179 Of The Kölnische Zeitung** (in Marx and Engels: **On Religion**, Progress Publishers, Moscow, 1957), pp. 32-33.

scripture, and is largely limited to expressing learned opinions in matters in which scripture is ambiguous or silent. These opinions may frequently conflict, and no great inconvenience is seen in this, since in such matters the operative principle by which a conclusion is reached is that of the consensus (*'ijma*) of the entire community, ascertained by consultation (*shura*).

In short, the relationship between the religious leadership and the community of the faithful in Sunni Islam is very different from that which obtains in Roman Catholicism. (There is a closer analogy in the case of Shi'a Islam, in which the religious leaders (*mullahs*) enjoy far more authority than their Sunni counterparts and are hierarchically organised, and where the principle of consensus is far less important than that of authoritative interpretation. But we are not dealing with Shi'a Islam.) Because of this difference, the relationship between the religious leadership and the state in Algeria also differs sharply from the Irish case.

It is not the case that Islam, or any more or less organised tendency within it, exercises the kind of conscious, purposeful, coherent and constant hegemony over state and society in Algeria that the Catholic hierarchy has exercised and continues to exercise in Southern Ireland. It was, perhaps, conceivable that the *'Ulama* might aspire to the exercise of such hegemony in the independent state, as the *mullahs* appear to be doing with success in Iran. Unlike their Iranian counterparts, however, the Algerian *'Ulama*, despite playing a substantial role in the genesis of Algerian nationalism, at no stage succeeded in constituting the political leadership of the national revolution and since Independence they have been obliged to accept a subordinate and dependent position *vis-à-vis* the political leadership. The Ministry of Religious Affairs in Algiers is the institutional expression and the organisational instrument of the hegemony of the state over the religious sphere, not of religion over the political sphere. In the Irish Republic, the Catholic hierarchy has never brooked the slightest interference in its affairs (and it alone decides what are 'its affairs') on the part of the political leadership of the state, and this autonomy has been the precondition of its hegemony over the politicians. In Algeria, on the other hand, the religious leaders collectively have little or no practical autonomy of the political leadership. In so far as they constitute an organised force, this is principally in virtue of their orchestration by the state, which pays their salaries and supervises their activities. Official Islam is precisely *"the cult of the will of the government"*.

In short, in Ireland the politicians are shepherded by the Church; in Algeria, the men of religion are kept men, and shepherded by the state. In Ireland, insufficiently docile politicians have been dealt with by the Church, notably Noel Browne, who as Minister of Health in 1951 was so rash as to introduce a modest venture in welfare provision (the *"Mother and Child"* scheme) without sounding the hierarchy's views first. In Algeria, insufficiently docile *'ulama* are dealt with by the State, notably Shaikh Abdellatif Soltani, who died under house arrest in 1984.

It follows from this that the state in Algeria has had the power to provide for and guarantee the position of religious minorities, whereas the state in Southern Ireland has never had this power. The Protestant community in the Irish Republic has been subject to the same laws as the Catholic majority, and these laws conform strictly to Catholic doctrine. Divorce and abortion are illegal for Protestants as well as Catholics in Southern Ireland. But the freedom of the Algerian state from religious supervision has enabled it to depart from strict Islamic law in much of its social legislation. A very great deal of legislation in Algeria is of modern European (and particularly French) origin. The characteristically Islamic ban on alcohol is not enforced. (Alcohol is difficult to obtain in some parts of Algeria, but it is not illegal to consume it and it is sold under licence in all the main towns.) And the severe punishments with which Islamic law is frequently identified in the West (the *hudud*, i.e., stoning, flogging, amputation, etc.) are quite unthinkable in Algeria. They are entirely absent from the penal code. As for divorce, this is already permitted by Islamic law in any case. Nor is contraception prohibited, as it was in Southern Ireland. (If the Algerian Government has been slow to promote *"family planning"* and has only recently begun to do so, this is not because it has had Islamic doctrine to get round, but because it has been afraid to affront a deep-seated popular prejudice in favour of large families and an even deeper-seated resistance to state interference in what is regarded as the entirely private domain of family life. That is a completely different matter.)

☆

It may be objected that much of this argument relies on hindsight and that the Algerian state has turned out to be less Islamic than one might very reasonably have expected, and that it was entirely reasonable of the Europeans to fear the worst. Conversely, one might wish to argue that the Irish state has turned out to be more strictly Catholic than could reasonably have been anticipated, that the Ulster Protestants did not have good grounds for expecting what has, in fact, occurred in the Republic, that it would therefore have been more rational of them to have gone quietly and ever hopefully into an all-Ireland Catholic state, and that their actual refusal to do this was irrational.

If one is determined at all costs to uphold the standard English prejudice that Ulster Protestants are mindless bigots, one might very well see virtue in such reasoning and try it on. But only political nonsense can come from this argument, even if it were not groundless, which it is. The overall point at issue, after all, is not whether or not the Ulster Protestants were justified in their resistance to Catholic nationalism a hundred years ago or in 1920, but whether or not they are justified in this resistance today. And the fact that their 19th century forefathers accurately predicted what has since come to pass in the South is certainly a very strong argument in vindication of their present position.

But the argument is groundless in any case. The nature of the social influence of Islam and its relationship to the state in independent Algeria is something which could certainly have been broadly predicted well before 1962, for the simple reason that it is, in its main features, inherent in the nature of Sunni Islam. And the same applies to Irish Catholicism, the main elements of which were clearly visible by the First Vatican Council in 1870, if not before. And the nature of the relationship between the Church and the political leadership of the nationalist movement was also clear from the fall of Parnell onwards, and became ever more visible in 1918.

This point can only be reinforced when the international dimension is taken into account. If the Catholic Church in Ireland was a purely national church, and enjoyed the kind of national autonomy over its internal affairs and matters of doctrine that most Protestant churches take for granted, its hegemony over the state might have proved short-lived. It is likely that it would have been obliged to reflect or at least accommodate the peculiarities, complexities and imperfections of Irish society to a substantial extent and scale down its ambitions to remould this society in accordance with its comprehensive social doctrine. And this state of affairs might have created opportunities for the more robust elements of the political establishment to assert themselves against the hierarchy, since they could claim to be equally well placed to interpret the current temper of the society and the national interest. The development of a clear dichotomy between religion and politics, church and state would then have been a serious prospect, and one which would have offered substantial hope to religious minorities and valid arguments to those who would allay their fears.

But this is not the actual state of affairs at all. The Catholic Church in Ireland is not a national church, it is the Irish detachment of the Universal Church militant which has its headquarters in the Vatican and proclaims its obedience to an infallible pope. And this state of affairs greatly reinforces the position of the hierarchy *vis-à-vis* the political leadership of the Republic. For what is or might be at issue between them is not the nature and needs of the society, which the latter could (if it dared) claim to be as well placed to gauge as the former, but the nature and implications of instructions in spiritual and doctrinal matters (including matters of social doctrine) received from Rome. And in this the hierarchy is evidently at a very great advantage, for it is the privileged recipient of these instructions, yet the political leaders owe no less obedience to the Holy Father than the members of the hierarchy themselves.

The international character of the Roman Catholic Church, together with the reassertion of the doctrine of papal infallibility since the First Vatican Council in 1870, has given enormous moral support to the ambition of the Irish hierarchy to ensure that the Irish Republic is governed in accordance with strict Catholic doctrine and to remould the society to this end. And it has maintained the members of the Irish political establishment in a state of permanent moral and ideological tutelage under their lords spiritual.

There is no parallel to this in Algerian Islam. The *'ulama* cannot invoke the authority of an external, international or supra-national, arbiter or fountain-head of doctrine in a bid to assert their claims against those of the state. Mecca does not have the authority of Rome and the regular conferences of Islamic heads of state have no authority. At the Islamic summit conference at Lahore in 1974, the Algerian President, Houari Boumediene, told the assembled faithful that, in his opinion as a good Muslim, *"verses from the Quran will not fill an empty stomach"*. Can one imagine Eamon de Valera (let alone Garret FitzGerald) expressing comparable sentiments in Rome?

It will no doubt be regarded as in extremely bad taste to have mentioned the international character of the Roman Catholic Church and its implications. England won its battle against the papacy so long ago that its intelligentsia appears to have no memory of it. And these days, *bienpensant* English intellectuals, who would not hesitate to chaff their Communist Party dinner companions for taking their line from Moscow, will freely deride the Ulster Protestant's dark mutterings about *"Rome rule"* and convince themselves that there is nothing in it, with a kind of liberal-ecumenical *pudeur*.

☆

If the Ulster Protestants were able, as a matter of demonstrable fact, to form an accurate estimate of what incorporation under a Home Rule government or an independent Irish state would mean, this is because they were already an extremely coherent community whose political, religious and intellectual leaders had been accustomed since the 17th century to pay close attention to developments within Irish Catholicism. The panic-stricken, if not hysterical, response of the Europeans in colonial Algeria to the predicament they found themselves in had a lot to do with the fact that they were a comparatively incoherent community whose leaders had rarely taken any interest in Algerian Muslim society (let alone developments within Algerian Islam) and were, by and large, comprehensively ignorant of it.

This is a difference between Ulster and Algeria on which the opponents of the Union and the supporters of the Anglo-Irish Agreement would prefer not to dwell. It is, in fact, the heart of the matter.

The French In Algeria

The French community in Algeria numbered a little short of one million in 1962, out of a total population of about ten million. But the Frenchness of this community was a rather abstract affair. In part, it was political, a function of the possession of citizenship of the one and indivisible French Republic, a citizenship denied to the Muslims. But the actual political life of the French in Algeria was substantially separate from that of the metropolis, so that citizenship of the latter was, in turn, a highly abstract matter. Mainly, this Frenchness was cultural. But this cultural Frenchness defined itself negatively, not positively. The Frenchness of the French in Algeria was a function, above all, of the fact that they were not Arabs or Muslims. It could not define itself positively, because of the considerable heterogeneity of the French community.

Only about 40 per cent of this community was of metropolitan French extraction. There was a very strong Spanish element, particularly in western Algeria, where colonial villages bore names like Rio Salado and the city of Oran was renowned for the fact that it *"kept Spanish hours"*. But it was also present in Algiers, where men with names such Ortiz and Perez were prominent among the die-hards in 1960-2. There was also a very important Corsican element, as well as considerable numbers of Italians and Maltese. A small but visible Alsatian community was also present, descended from some 5,000 refugees who had fled *"the German embrace"* in 1870 and had settled in eastern Algeria, in townships bearing names such as Strasbourg and Metz. Contemporary academic Marxism has them to thank for Louis Althusser. There were also a number of Bretons, one of whom married a Spanish woman named Sintes; their son was Albert Camus. And, of course, there were the Jews, who had been in Algeria since the 3rd century AD, and thus long before the arrival of the Arabs in the 7th century, and who were gradually assimilated into the European community after 1870.

The cultural diversity of this population in respect of religion and language (not to mention dress, cuisine, indeed life-style in general) did not, in itself, preclude it from developing into a coherent community. Nearly all modern nations are mongrels, after all, and none more so than the British, as Irish nationalists have frequently pointed out. The same is evidently true of

France, which has developed as a nation out of all kinds of bits and pieces (Celtic, Roman, Teutonic, etc.,). But the European population in Algeria could have cohered only around its French nucleus, that is, the element of metropolitan French origin. Like the English in America, this was the first element to settle in Algeria, and it was also the largest.

Had this element been able to put down strong roots in Algeria and carve out a distinct place for itself there, it might have been able eventually to envisage a distinct destiny for the European population of Algeria as a whole, to take the lead in realising this destiny, and to enable this population to cohere, economically, culturally and politically, by associating its diverse other elements in this common destiny. But this French element was, in fact, quite unable to perform the role which the English nucleus has historically performed in America. It was inhibited from doing so by the character of its original relationship to the French state, a relationship which was dependent in the extreme, and from which it never emancipated itself.

The original settlement of Algeria resembled that of Australia rather than that of America. It was not the work of voluntary emigrants, who represented the most robustly independent and ideologically advanced elements of the metropolitan society, and who had chosen to make a new life in a new world, in order to be free to live by their own lights. It was the work of the French state, which realised by the mid-1840s that large-scale settlement was needed to consolidate the conquest which was being achieved by force of arms. The settlers were social and national flotsam and jetsam, paupers, refugees or other truculent elements who were shovelled out by the thousand, notably the defeated Republican workers from Paris after the abortive rising of 1848. And their arrival and settlement in Algeria was supervised by the military authorities.

From 1830 to 1870 French Algeria was under military rule. The state which had launched the conquest, the Bourbon monarchy, was swept away a few weeks later in the 1830 Revolution which brought the *"Citizen King"*, Louis Philippe, to the throne. It was under him that the conquest of the Algerian interior was undertaken in earnest from 1840 onwards, and the policy of settlement decided upon. The advent of the Second Empire in 1851 eventually led to a change in perspective. Louis Bonaparte was as hostile to the settlers as they were to him, and he sought to govern Algeria, not as an integral part of France but as an *"Arab kingdom"*. This tentative development of a constructive and implicitly pro-Muslim colonial policy came to an end with the fall of the Second Empire in September 1870.

With the advent of the Third Republic, the settlers secured civilian government for the colony, which was now integrated as three *départements* of the French Republic. The tendency of the military administration had been to protect Muslim interests to some extent, once the work of *"pacification"* had been accomplished. The end of military government left the Muslims at the mercy of the settlers. But if the settlers had freed themselves from military supervision, they had by no mean emancipated themselves from the French state. On the contrary, they remained as dependent as ever on the metropolis in every respect, economically, militarily and politically. The advent of civilian administration in no way implied self-government, let alone autonomy in any broader sense.

The fact that Australia was the other side of the world from the mother country made it inconceivable that it should be treated as an integral part of the United Kingdom. And this state of affairs made it possible for a British settler community, which closely resembled its Algerian counterpart in certain subjective respects, to develop a distinctive collective identity and the ability and will to go its own way. The fact that Algeria, while in a different continent, was (by comparison with Australia) fairly close to the mother country, and that, in particular, there was no intervening land-mass between it and France, meant that it was just possible for the French to treat it as an overseas extension of the metropolis, and to declare, with that superb disdain for practical obstacles for which they are so widely admired, that *"the Mediterranean runs through France like the Seine through Paris"*.

But this state of affairs, while apparently advantageous to the French settlers in the short run, doomed them in the long run. It made the Australian line of development impossible, not that this line of development had ever been more than the most implausible and abstract possibility in the first place, given the size, cultural cohesion and combativity of the indigenous population.

☆

From 1870 onwards there was a fundamental incoherence in the French position in Algeria. The country was not regarded as a colony but as an integral part of France, yet, while it was represented in the National Assembly in Paris, it had its own colonial administration, with a Governor-General and a set of specific, indeed unique, institutions of representation and local government. It was most certainly not administered like any other region of France. Moreover, the Muslim majority were not citizens, but subjects. They could only acquire French citizenship if they agreed to abandon their legal status as Muslims and thus the particular rights they possessed under Islamic law. Only a tiny handful were willing to take this step.

With the benefit of hindsight, it can be seen that France had only four coherent options after 1840. These were:
(i) to make *"l'Algérie francaise"* a reality by extending full citizenship to the Muslims, making the necessary special dispensation in respect of their personal juridical status;
(ii) to make *"l'Algérie francaise"* a reality by assimilating the Muslims culturally as a prerequisite of integrating them politically, an enterprise which would have entailed a frontal and protracted assault on their Islamic faith;
(iii) to govern the place as a colony and not pretend that it was, or could become, part of the Republic, an option which meant keeping the settlers disenfranchised in the short term and endeavouring to phase them out gently in the long term;
(iv) to get out.

The tragedy is that France did none of these things. No doubt the incessant political turmoil in the metropolis which was unleashed in 1789 and brought to an end only by the Fifth Republic in 1958 made it impossible for Paris to pursue a consistently intelligent colonial policy. If we accept that options (i) and (ii) were not on politically, that leaves only (iii) and (iv) as coherent possibilities. The much-maligned Louis Bonaparte went for something approaching (iii). It was the only time Paris had a coherent policy, until de Gaulle went for (iv) in 1960.

☆

The fact that the European society in Algeria was a creature of the French state made it inconceivable that this society would acquire a realistic appreciation of its situation and negotiate a durable *modus vivendi* with the Muslim population. It existed under the umbrella of the state. The state guaranteed its privileged position in Algeria as a society of full citizens in a sea of oppressed subjects, and the state mediated, and thereby obscured, its relationship with these subjects.

In so far as the French community in Algeria had traditions of suspicion of and hostility towards successive liberal governments in Paris, these traditions did not dispose or equip it to assert its independence of Paris and make its own way in the world. They disposed it to seek the overthrow of the existing government in Paris and its replacement by a more amenable one. At no point did the French community in Algeria attempt to make itself the master of its own destiny. In this, it was very like every other provincial segment of the metropolitan French population. It was the product of the *étatiste* tradition. It had the mark of that tradition upon it. It knew how to hustle votes and muster majorities in the National Assembly in order to bring a government down, and it knew how to riot in Algiers or Oran to the same end. But it did not know how to fend for itself. It had never needed to fend for itself before 1960, when it became clear what de Gaulle had in mind. And by that late stage, there was no time for it to acquire the necessary knowledge. It could think of nothing better than to try to repeat its exploit of May 1958, that is, to unseat de Gaulle and replace him with someone else. In other words, when the French state finally made up its mind to negotiate with the Muslim rebellion, there was nothing the *"colons"* could do except submit to the *fait accompli* or endeavour desperately to sabotage it.

France created the settler community in Algeria, and France pulled the rug out from under it. It unmade what it had made. And democracy had as little to do with the ultimate act of destruction as it had with the original act of creation. *"Raison d'état* gave birth to the French settlement in Algeria, and *"raison d'état"* signed its death warrant. Its end was in its beginning.

With the British community in Northern Ireland it is another story altogether.

The Protestants In Ulster

British intellectuals and politicians and leader-writers who rely for their understanding of Northern Ireland on half-recollected phrases from their school history books about the *"Plantation of Ulster"* may be forgiven for supposing that the Protestant community there resembles its French counterpart in Algeria in that it, too, had its origin in an act of government policy and *"raison d'état"*. But this supposition is entirely mistaken.

What determined the character of the French community in Algeria was not only its origin in an act of policy by the French state, but the fact that it never ceased to be dependent upon the French state, and that the dependent character of its relationship with the state was not significantly affected by the periodic political upheavals in the metropolis. The *étatiste* tradition inherited from the Absolutist monarchy was not overthrown by the Revolution of 1789 but reinforced by it, notably in the Jacobin dictatorship, and was subsequently confirmed, rationalised and codified under Napoleon. Thereafter, the form of government of the state underwent repeated change, but the essential nature of the relationship between state and society survived unaltered. The state, whether Republic or Empire, maintained a highly centralised bureaucracy and a large standing army. It regularly employed the latter to suppress unrest. It possessed both the means and the will to coerce the society, it mediated the relations between both the social classes and the regional sections of the population in the most regular and visible manner, and inhibited the development of autonomous political reflexes in all sections of the population.

The British state which fathered the *"Plantation"* of Ulster disappeared not long afterwards. The first plantation in Ireland occurred in the South, in Munster, in the reign of Elizabeth I. The plantation of Ulster occurred in 1609-10, under James I. British political development entered its absolutist phase under the Tudors and this continued under the Stuarts. But absolutism in Great Britain was prevented from consolidating itself. Unlike its French counterpart, it did not give birth to an enduring *étatiste* tradition, because it was cut short in its prime. The English Revolution was, in essence, a revolution against absolutism. The Civil War was won by the Parliamentary forces, and although this victory gave rise to a dictatorial regime under Cromwell (the Protectorate), based on the New Model Army, this development was extremely short-lived. It did not survive Cromwell's death. The New Model Army, which had been politically radical, was detested by the bourgeoisie and was disbanded shortly after the restoration of the monarchy in 1660. Thereafter the state lacked the means to engage in general coercion of the society in the furtherance of policy, a point which Karl Marx emphasised when he came to consider the prospects for the socialist movement in Great Britain in the 1870s. And the Revolution of 1688 finally established the supremacy of Parliament *vis-à-vis* the Crown and the conditional, constitutional, character of the monarchy.

What this means is that the nature of the British state underwent a fundamental change in the decades following the plantation of Ulster. It ceased to be a state capable of dealing with the society in a high-handed manner or of promoting developments for which the society was not yet ready. It was unable to sustain the plantation settlements where these proved unable to sustain themselves and it was unable to supervise or constrain them where they prospered and developed a will of their own. The plantation of Munster failed. And several plantation settlements on the southern and western fringes of Ulster also failed, in the case of the latter, despite their proximity to the town of Londonderry, which was the official centre of the Plantation. But the majority of the plantation settlements in Ulster survived and consolidated themselves and evolved into a single, unified and coherent community. They did this without the aid or prompting of an overseer state. But their efforts in this respect were enormously reinforced by the presence in Ulster of a Protestant community which had never been part of the Plantation, which had established itself unaided and which was accordingly able to function as the nucleus of an increasingly coherent and self-reliant community there.

The core of Protestant Ulster are the counties of Antrim and Down. These were not included in the Plantation, because they were already in the process of being settled when the policy of Plantation was decided upon by the British Crown. The settlers were independent, voluntary, migrants from the Scottish Lowlands, particularly the western districts of Ayrshire and Galloway. And they were Protestants, which is to say that in their faith, general outlook and motivation they were quite unlike the transported settlers in Australia and Algeria, and very like the first English settlers in America.

There was nothing new about movements of population between Ireland and Scotland. The idea that the narrow strip of sea between the two constituted an obstacle to communication (let alone a cultural or political frontier) is an illusion of hindsight. The development of modern road and rail transport has overcome all the natural obstacles to overland travel which daunted previous ages. But in the 16th and 17th centuries, short-range sea travel was often far easier than travel overland. Migrations between Ireland and Scotland had been occurring regularly, in both directions, for many hundreds of years. There had been an Ulster Gaelic colonisation of the Scottish Highlands, and overlapping Gaelic kingdoms between Ireland and Scotland had been the rule. The Lowland Scots who settled in Antrim and Down in the first years of the 17th century were not regarded as foreign invaders by the local Gaelic population, as the French were regarded by the Arabs and Berbers of Algeria. They settled where they did with the agreement of the local Gaelic chieftains. What distinguished this migration from its predecessors, however, was the fact that the migrants were Protestants.

The cultural division between the Protestant, English-speaking Lowlands and the Catholic, Gaelic-speaking Highlands was already well established in Scotland by the end of the 16th century. The effect of the migration of Lowland Scots to Ulster, together with the mainly English settlers of the Plantation, was to establish the same cultural division in the North of Ireland. (The same division later developed, although in a somewhat different way, in Wales, which was Catholic and a bastion of the Royalists in the Civil War, but later evolved into a bastion of Non-conformist Protestantism, and social radicalism. Because it developed in a different way, the connection between the survival of the Celtic language and that of the Catholic faith was broken in Wales. Large parts of Wales remained Welsh-speaking when they underwent conversion to Protestantism and Welsh became a vehicle for the propagation of the new faith. As a result, Welsh has survived while Gaelic has practically disappeared from Scotland and Ireland.) This cultural division was not a national division in 16th and 17th century Scotland, which was a unified kingdom under the Stuart monarchy. Nor did it become a national division in Wales. Nor was it a national division in 17th century Ireland, which was in no sense a national unit prior to the settlement of Ulster. The national division which exists in Ireland today did not begin to develop until the second quarter of the 19th century.

Scottish Presbyterianism was in the vanguard of the Reformation and it remained in the vanguard of the development of democracy in Great Britain, contributing substantially to the Parliamentary side in the Civil War. The new Protestant community in Ulster quickly entered the vanguard of the democratic cause in the world at large. It participated actively in the Civil War on the Parliamentary side and again in the 1688 Revolution. It supported the American colonists in their war of independence against the British Crown and public festivities in support of the French Revolution were held in Belfast on the anniversary of the fall of the Bastille. And when the question of participating in the lucrative slave trade was discussed by leading Belfast capitalists in 1786, it was agreed to have nothing to do with it, on the grounds that *"the trade in men"* was against their Christian principles.

If this society, with political traditions such as these, is now regarded by English liberal and left-wing intellectuals as the last word in bigoted reaction, this is in part because it has been systematically confused with the very different Protestant community in southern Ireland. This confusion has been assiduously cultivated and exploited by Irish Republicanism.

The Protestants in the South were the Anglo-Irish gentry. They were a class, not a community. They were the great landowners in southern Ireland and they monopolised the offices of state and the professions. Their Protestantism was very different from that which predominated in the North. It was that of the Church of Ireland, that is, the Irish branch of Anglicanism, the religion of the British establishment. In doctrine, social outlook and social basis it was far removed from the dissenter Protestantism of Ulster and, as elsewhere in the Brtish isles, existed in a relationship of reciprocal suspicion, if not hostility, with it.

To say that the Anglo-Irish were a class in southern Ireland is misleading, however, in that it suggests that southern Ireland was a coherent class society like, for instance, contemporary England. In reality, it was entirely different. The Anglo-Irish were rather a colonial ruling caste, superimposed upon the culturally quite separate society of the Gaelic clansmen beneath. Following the flight to Europe of the old clan aristocracy in the 17th century, the Gaels were reduced to an oppressed peasantry of tenant farmers on the estates of the Anglo-Irish gentry, and subject to the system known as rack-renting, whereby any increase in the productivity of their farms was simply creamed off in higher rents. The history of southern Ireland is essentially the story of how these downtrodden Gaels taught themselves English, were mobilised by Daniel O'Connell in the 1820s in the cause of Catholic Emancipation, embarked upon a vigorous class-struggle against their landlords between 1850 and 1890 and, under the banner of Catholic nationalism, developed into a fully fledged society of their own, sloughing off the parasitic colonial caste above them in the process.

The Anglo-Irish are often referred to as the Protestant Ascendancy. This is an entirely accurate name for them. But it properly refers to them alone. It does not refer, and was not actually used to refer, to the quite separate Protestant community in Ulster, which was not a caste or a class, still less an exploitative or parasitic one, but a coherent society in its own right, within which all the social classes characteristic of bourgeois society had developed. In 1982, a feature film was made about the events in Northern Ireland. It was called **Ascendancy**. Its title was a travesty of the historical character of the Protestant community in Ulster and of the nature of its relationship with the Catholic population. It received the standard enthusiastic reviews in the magazines of the British intelligentsia.

The capitalist development of Ulster was not based on the colonial exploitation of a downtrodden Catholic population. It was based on a vigorous class struggle *within* the Protestant community. Protestant tenant farmers were subjectively in a very different position from the demoralised Gaels in the south. The democratic and individualist elements of their Protestant culture disposed them to assert their rights. They confronted their Protestant landlords and won a fundamental concession from them, a form of land tenure known as *"Ulster Custom"* which gave them substantial property rights in their tenancies and an interest in developing them. In sharp contrast to the South, where rack-renting inhibited capitalist economic development, in the North a modern and vigorous capitalist agriculture slowly emerged and with it the economic and social basis for the subsequent industrialisation of the province. This capitalist development occurred without any help from the British state. All the capital inflows into Ireland in the 18th century were directed to the South. The policy of the British government was to foster capitalist development in the South. This policy failed because the social basis for a firmly grounded capitalist development did not exist in the South. It only came into existence in the second half of the 19th century.

A substantial capitalist development occurred in Ulster because the social pre-conditions for this development were generated within the Protestant community there. Belfast developed as a major city in the course of the industrial revolution. The industrial revolution occurred in Northern Ireland at the same time and in the same way as it occurred in the north of England and Clydeside. The development of Belfast kept pace with, and closely resembled, the development of Liverpool, Manchester and Glasgow.

The fact that Belfast is the political and economic capital of Northern Ireland is, in itself, a clear indicator of the independent nature of the processes of social development which have taken place there since 1610. The town which was designated by the British Crown to be the capital of the Plantation was Londonderry. Londonderry was a colonial creation like Dublin, and like Algiers and Oran. There is no counter-part to Belfast in Algeria.

The entire economic and social history and character of the Protestant community in Ulster could not be more different from that of the European population in Algeria. Its relations with the Catholic population have, correspondingly, been entirely different from the Algerian *colons'* relations with the Muslims.

Settlers And Natives In Algeria

Muslim resistance to French rule was tribally-based throughout the 19th century. The modern anti-colonial movement only developed in the course of the First World War. It was modern in that it did not represent the interests of this or that tribe, but claimed and endeavoured to speak and act on behalf of the Muslim community as a whole.

The first movement to emerge was, nonetheless, quite unrepresentative of the Muslim population as a whole. It was based on the urban, and part of the rural, Muslim elite, in particular those elements which had received French education. It did not oppose French rule, but merely sought political rights for Muslims within the French Republic. It pressed these demands in an entirely constitutional and peaceful way, moreover. Yet it was met with the most uncompromising opposition on the part of the European settler community.

There can be no doubt that a tendency within metropolitan French politics was favourable to these moderate Muslim demands. Had it been possible to concede them, the prospect of eventually integrating the entire Muslim population into the French body politic would have been a realistic possibility. And such a development would have profoundly consolidated Algeria's constitutional position as an integral part of the French Republic and would thereby have guaranteed the long-term interests of the Europeans in Algeria.

In the event, these demands were not conceded, and an entirely different tendency developed within Muslim politics, seeking a radical separatist solution to the problem of Muslim disenfranchisement in Algeria. It was not possible to concede them because successive governments in Paris during the Third Republic were based on fragile parliamentary coalitions and frequently depended upon the votes of the Algerian settlers' representatives. These settler deputies in the National Assembly acted as a bloc and consistently thwarted proposals for reform in Algeria.

The fact that the Algerian settlers behaved in this way is not disputed by anyone these days, and for our present purposes it is sufficient to state this fact in order to be in a position to highlight the entirely different political behaviour of the Ulster Protestants. But some words of explanation of the Algerian settlers' behaviour may nonetheless be in order. For, in retrospect at any rate, this behaviour appears to have been entirely suicidal, and it is difficult for the detached observer to suppress the feeling that such suicidal behaviour was absurd, and that those who indulged in it simply got their just deserts in 1962.

The apparently absurd refusal to countenance reform in the Muslim interest is to be explained, in essence, by the combination of two factors. First, it is necessary to realise that the politics of the Algerian settler community were dominated by the interests of a small class of agrarian magnates and merchants, which interests undoubtedly required the continued disenfranchisement of the Muslim population. Second, while the vast majority of the settlers would not have been materially disadvantaged by the reforms in question, they were in no position to form an independent opinion of their interests in the matter.

Under colonial rule, a large sector of modern capitalist agriculture was developed in Algeria. But this sector did not develop on the basis of a society of small farmers, as capitalist agriculture developed in Northern Ireland and America. The majority of the settlers in Algeria did not have farming in their blood and soon abandoned their holdings. The introduction of viticulture in the 1890s encouraged this process, since it required substantial capital investment and thereby favoured a rapid process of concentration of landholdings. And the European sector of agriculture in the cereal belt of the interior, where yields were low and extensive farming the rule, was characterised by huge estates under the ownership of joint-stock companies from a very early stage. From the 1920s onwards, a general flight from the land took place. Thereafter, the small colon homesteader was a rarity. The vast majority of the settlers were concentrated in the coastal cities and were employed in the service sector. The agrarian interest was accordingly the interest of a small number of powerful magnates. The labour force they exploited was almost entirely Muslim. It consisted of recently proletarianised tribesmen, without any traditions of organised activity on the basis of class interest. Socially and politically they were docile in the extreme. Their European employers engaged in broadly paternalistic relations with them. They had every interest in preserving the docility of this workforcce and no interest in conceding political rights to it, especially since the members of this workforce were not demanding political rights.

The fact that Algeria was united with metropolitan France by a customs union, and that French capitalism was extremely backward by comparison with Britain and Germany, ensured that scarcely any industrial development occurred in Algeria during the colonial period. Neither a European industrial bourgeoisie developed nor a Muslim industrial proletariat. Unlike South Africa, where democratic reform in the interest of the Black working class has enjoyed the support of certain white industrialists (e.g., the Oppenheimers), there was no basis for such a development in Algeria.

Within Algeria up until 1937, Muslim anti-colonialism was based on the small traders and shop-keepers and petty intelligentsia of the small towns of the interior, especially in eastern Algeria, that is to say, on sections of the Muslim population with which the overwhelming majority of the European community in the coastal cities had little or no contact whatever. It was not based on the Muslim underclass of Algiers or Oran with which the *petits blancs* (poor whites) were familiar, nor did it seek or evoke support among the Muslim labourers on the large European farms. And when an explicitly separatist nationalism developed, it did so amongst the Algerian migrant workers in France. The revolutionary nationalist movement which eventually gave birth to the FLN in 1954 was pioneered by an organisation called the *Etoile Nord-Africaine* (North African Star). This was founded in Paris in 1926 and operated initially under the aegis of the French Communist Party. It was entirely based on the Algerian labour migrants in France. These migrants came overwhelmingly from the densely populated mountain zones of eastern Algeria, regions which had not attracted European settlement because of the abruptness of the relief and the poverty of the soil.

In short, Algerian nationalism developed almost entirely outside the field of vision of the European population. It was based on those sections of the Muslim population which had been least affected by European land appropriation and which engaged in little or no intercourse with the settler community. It was not until 1937 that the leader of the *Etoile*, Messali Hadj, founded a nationalist party in Algeria itself, the *Parti du Peuple Algerien* (PPA). This quickly acquired a following among the Muslims of Algiers, but it was banned on the outbreak of the Second World War, before it had had time to give serious food for thought to the European community.

With the resumption of normal political life in 1945, it can fairly be said that the European community in Algeria was entirely unaware of the political development which had taken place amongst the Muslims. It was in no position to realise that Messali's PPA enjoyed massive support amongst the labour migrants in France and equally massive support in the remote mountains of north-eastern Algeria where scarcely any settlers ever ventured. It was accordingly in no position to realise that it had every interest in dissociating itself from the policy of the agrarian magnates and in conceding democratic reform to the Muslims while there was still time. Even the abortive nationalist uprising of May 1945 failed to bring this home. The rising had been centred on the towns of Setif, Kherrata and Guelma in eastern Algeria, and based mainly in their mountainous environs; above all, it had gone off at half-cock, and appeared a very ragged affair. It was therefore assimilated by European opinion to the old tradition of localised tribal revolts, rather than recognised as a portent of things to come.

Only the French state was in a position to appreciate the overall political situation fully in the years preceding the outbreak of the war in 1954. But the Fourth Republic was essentially the same as the Third Republic. De Gaulle's proposals for a strong presidential regime capable of overriding special interests were rejected in 1946. And thereafter the government in Paris was at the mercy of shifting coalitions of deputies in the National Assembly, such that its Algerian policy could be determined by the settler bloc controlled by the agrarian interest. There was no force capable of educating the mass of the European settlers in Algiers and Oran in the elementary political realities of the situation. Even the outbreak of the war itself was unable to do this, because it was largely confined to the remote mountain regions of eastern Algeria until 1957. And by then, it was far too late to envisage any alternative to Algerian independence.

Thus, even if the European community in Algeria had not been heterogeneous and incoherent, and congenitally dependent upon the French state, it is difficult to envisage how it might have been enabled to acquire more foresight and realism in time for it to devise an escape route from its predicament other than the one which de Gaulle ultimately imposed upon it.

It is an illusion of detached intellectuals with no understanding of the actual politics of the situation to suppose that the Europeans of Algeria displayed a suicidal blindness to the reality of their predicament. The only part of Muslim Algeria which was visible to them until it was too late was an entirely innocuous part. It was the hidden Muslim Algeria of the Atlas mountains which did them in. And they were in no position to gauge the threat to them until this threat had been put into effect. Like the Titanic, the European community in Algeria only noticed the submerged nine-tenths of the iceberg which sunk it when the fatal collision had already occurred.

No democrat can regret the victory of the Algerian Muslims in winning the right to determine their own political future. And the argument that the liquidation of the European community in Algeria was inevitable sooner or later is probably unanswerable. But only someone who is devoid of imagination and insensible to human suffering can approve of the way in which this community was liquidated. And only someone who is accustomed to passing moral judgement and sentence of death on communities he knows nothing of could be capable of recommending that the abrupt and traumatic fate of the Europeans of Algeria be deliberately visited upon communities elsewhere.

Such a recommendation is, in any case, peculiarly inapposite where the Protestants of Northern Ireland are concerned. They have long possessed a most intimate and comprehensive knowledge of the various political tendencies within the Catholic community in Ireland. And they have repeatedly given their full support to the cause of democratic reform in the interests of this community. It is the British political establishment whose behaviour has been characterised by blindness and contempt for democratic principle, not the Protestants of Ulster.

Settlers And Natives In Ireland

The question of democratic reform in the interests of the Catholic population of Ireland first became an issue in the last quarter of the 18th century. It was raised by the most far-sighted tendency in the southern Protestant Ascendancy, but failed to elicit significant support within the Ascendancy caste as a whole. But it elicited general and vigorous support from the Ulster Protestant community.

By the 1770s, the Protestant landlord Ascendancy in the South had had everything its own way for nearly a century. The Catholic Gaels were a downtrodden and demoralised mass. The political substance of the old Gaelic clan society had been irrevocably crippled by the defeat of the clan aristocracy in the 17th century. The Gaelic nobles in the North of Ireland had been crushed in 1603, when their leader, Hugh O'Neill, finally surrendered to the Crown following his unsuccessful rebellion. In 1607, unable to endure the life of a vassal, O'Neill, who held the position under the Crown of Earl of Tyrone, fled to Europe together with O'Donnell, the Earl of Tyrconnell and a number of lesser nobles, an event known to history as the Flight of the Earls. And after the decisive defeat of the Stuarts in 1688-90, the rest of the old aristocracy of Gaelic Ireland followed suit, in what is popularly known as the Flight of the Wild Geese. Thereafter, Gaelic Ireland was leaderless. The fragmentation of Gaelic society by the clan structure, which had previously been the counterpart of its vigour, persisted long after the flight of the nobles, but served merely to inhibit the development of a new, collective, sense of identity and common interest.

From 1688 onwards, the political monopoly of the landlord Ascendancy was expressed in its domination of the Irish Parliament, in which neither Catholics nor the dissenter Protestants of Ulster were represented. By the 1770s, some Ascendancy politicians realised that this monopoly could not last, and sought to guarantee the position of the southern Protestants by getting them to act as the nucleus of an Irish nation composed of the Catholics and the Ulster Protestants as well as the Ascendancy caste. The leader of this tendency was Henry Grattan. Having mobilised the Ascendancy behind him in a campaign to get Westminster to concede legislative independence to the Irish Parliament (which was in fact conceded in 1782), Grattan then proposed to make the Irish Parliament the instrument for the process of national development he had in mind, by a programme of democratic electoral reform, including the admission of Catholics to the franchise. At this point Grattan lost most of his following among the southern Protestants. The Ascendancy Parliament refused to reform itself. But Grattan's programme was vigorously supported by the Ulster Protestants, including its provision for admission of Catholics to the franchise. It was this support for democratic reform which underlay the development of the United Irishmen.

The core of the United Irishmen was Protestant Ulster, and the social basis of the movement was Antrim and Down, and particularly the city of Belfast itself. But the immediate political basis of the movement was a development analogous to the Minutemen in the rebel American colonies, the Irish Volunteers. The Volunteers had been set up initially as an entirely defensive move without political motives. France was in alliance with the American colonists in the 1770s and a French attack on Great Britain, and especially in its Irish rear, was feared by the authorities. (A rather halfhearted French assault did in fact take place, at Carrickfergus in Antrim.) In the South, the Volunteers were controlled by the Ascendancy gentry, and consisted essentially of their personal retainers. But in the North, the Volunteers were democratically organised and were under the control of no landed class; they were the people in arms.

Once the Volunteers had emerged as a force, Grattan used them to threaten the Westminster Parliament with, in order to wring from it the concession of legislative independence for the Irish Parliament. When he subsequently lost the support of the southern Ascendancy for his programme of admitting Catholics to the franchise, this programme was taken up by the Ulster detachments of the Volunteers, together with the demand for a radical democratic reform of the franchise in general - the ending of *"rotten boroughs"* and so on — on which Grattan himself was less keen. When it appeared that the Westminster Parliament was going to interfere in Ireland on the side of the corrupt Ascendancy Parliament and against the movement for democratic reform, a tendency developed within the Volunteers prepared to contemplate separation from Great Britain, since this seemed to be the prerequisite of democratic change. This tendency was greatly stimulated by the French Revolution. From 1791, the **Northern Star**, the paper of the United Irishmen in Belfast, devoted half of its columns to the most detailed coverage of political developments in France. The hostility of the British establishment to the triumph of revolutionary democracy in France only served to reinforce the separatist inclinations of the radical democrats in Belfast.

In the event, Westminster began to change its attitude to the southern Ascendancy. In 1793, William Pitt forced the Irish Parliament to agree to admit Catholics to the franchise. (Not all Catholics were admitted, of course; the franchise remained a property franchise. But it was much broader than the property franchise in Great Britain and it no longer discriminated against Catholics, merely the lower classes in general.) This change in British policy, together with the deterioration of revolutionary politics in France (the increasingly indefensible Reign of Terror, followed by the Directory), led a significant element in Ulster Protestant opinion to change its mind about the case for separation from the British Crown, and when the radical separatist wing of the United Irishmen finally launched its revolt in 1798, it no longer represented the mainstream of Ulster Protestant opinion, and the revolt failed.

Within two years, in 1800, the Act of Union incorporated Ireland as a whole into the United Kingdom and the Irish Parliament in Dublin was abolished. And since Westminster seemed resolved at last on a policy of progressive reform in Ireland, and was no longer engaged in propping up the corrupt Ascendancy in the South, the Protestants of Ulster decided that their own democratic objectives would be best served by the Union, and the separatist perspective was comprehensively abandoned.

(Southern Irish nationalism, which is comprehensively and militantly Catholic at home but understands the need to play this down for external consumption and present a democratic and even secular face to the world, is quite incapable of making sense of the political behaviour of Protestant Ulster between 1790 and 1810. It needs to pretend that there is only one Irish nation, and that this nation has existed since the year dot, and that the true interests of this nation have always required separation from Great Britain, and that the Ulster Protestants are really Irishmen, and that in 1798 they actually behaved as real Irishmen in so far as they took up arms against the British Crown. It constantly denounces the political behaviour of the Protestants of Ulster since 1800 as an unprincipled betrayal of the nationalist ideals of the United Irishmen revolt of 1798. It is incapable of recognising that the substance of those ideals was not nationalism, as this is understood by the Catholic nationalist tradition, but democratic reform. In late 18th century France, *"la nation"* did not mean the French as opposed to, say, the Germans, it meant the people as opposed to the aristocracy. It was a popular, democratic, idea. It had nothing to do with the cultivation of cultural peculiarities, and everything to do with democratic reform. There is a *"Place de la Nation"* in Paris. It is in the heart of what used to be known as the *"red belt"*, and is one of the traditional meeting places of the French Left. If the United Irishmen spoke of *"the nation"*, they meant by this exactly what the French revolutionaries they so admired meant by it, the democratic cause of the people against the corrupt landlord class. Protestant Ulster was remaining entirely true to the substance of the ideals of 1798 in supporting the Union after 1800.)

Protestant Ulster's support for democratic reform in the Catholic interest did not peter out after 1800. The admission of Catholics to the franchise in 1793 fell short of total Catholic emancipation from the old penal laws, for Catholics were still barred from sitting in Parliament. This was the issue which Daniel O'Connell took up as the main plank of his Catholic Emancipation movement in the 1820s. O'Connell enjoyed the support of Protestant Ulster. (There was a tendency in Ulster which had reservations about this reform, because the nature of O'Connell's agitation was already Catholic-nationalist in substance, and this tendency had an inkling of where this movement would eventually go. But the members of this tendency swallowed their own pragmatic reservations and supported the Emancipation movement, because their own democratic principles would not allow them not to do so.) Catholic Emancipation (the right of Catholics to sit in Parliament) was conceded by the Westminster Parliament in 1829. O'Connell promptly adopted the aim of the Repeal of the Union, and the Catholic nationalist movement was launched.

Nor did Ulster's support for reform in the interests of the Catholic population of Ireland come to an end in 1829. Crucial to the formation of the Catholic Irish nation was the struggle on the land between 1850 and 1890, in which the old rack-rented tenant farmers of the South at last took on their (now absentee) Anglo-Irish landlords and won, and became a substantial and self-confident class of independent farmers, and the core of the Catholic nation. This movement was launched by what were known as the *Tenant Leagues*. These leagues enjoyed a lot of popular support in Ulster. In fact, the first tenant leagues were founded in Ulster, by Protestant tenant farmers who felt the need to reassert the tenant-right (Ulster Custom) which they had already won, but which had never been given legal expression. These Protestant tenant-leagues were not only concerned with the particular interests of Protestant farmers in Ulster, however. They actively identified themselves with the cause of the tenant-farmers in the South, and expressed their solidarity in all kinds of practical ways. And when the outcome of the struggle in the South, in the tenants' favour, was at last ratified by the Westminster Parliament, in Balfour's *Land Purchase Act* of 1903, this was supported by the Ulster Unionist MPs. The idea that Ulster Unionism was based on a reactionary landlord interest has been much canvassed by Republican historiography, but it is without foundation.

In short, Protestant Ulster was from the first in the vanguard of the democratic movement and it supported every demand for progressive democratic reform in the Catholic interest from the 1770s to 1920. The one demand it did not support was the demand for the Repeal of the Union and, subsequently, for Home Rule, because the substance of these demands was Catholic-nationalist, not democratic. But the Ulster Protestants quickly dissociated themselves from the Anglo-Irish gentry who formed the Unionist opposition to Home Rule in the South. Thereafter, Ulster Unionism was concerned only with the right of the Northern Protestants to remain in the United Kingdom and did not oppose the claims of the Home Rule Party where the South was concerned. And in 1912, the Ulster Unionist MPs at Westminster offered to support Asquith's Third Home Rule Bill, on condition that it was amended so as to exclude the four overwhelmingly Protestant counties of the north-east of Ulster. The entire spirit of Ulster Unionism was to acknowledge the right of the Catholic South to go its own way, while simply insisting on the right of Protestant Ulster similarly to decide for itself what its political future should be. Ulster Unionism from early on willingly conceded the right of self-determination to the Catholic Irish population. The continuing drama in Northern Ireland today has everything to do with the fact that the Catholic-nationalist movement, from Parnell's Home Rule

Party, Arthur Griffith's Sinn Fein and De Valera's Fianna Fail to John Hume' SDLP and the Provisional IRA today, has never accepted that the Protestant community in Ulster was entitled to the same right of self-determination which it claimed for itself.

The same adherence to democratic political principles characterised the attitude of Ulster Unionism towards the Catholic minority in the North when Partition occurred. The last thing the Unionists sought was to set up an *"Orange state"* in which the Catholics would be an oppressed minority under Protestant rule. They were entirely opposed to any kind of state being set up in Northern Ireland, because they foresaw that it would be perceived by the Catholics as a Protestant state and that the Catholics would accordingly be alienated from it. No one was more representative of Ulster Unionism in the period from 1912 to 1920 than Sir Edward Carson. Carson was a vigorous opponent of Lloyd George's scheme to impose devolved government on Northern Ireland. This is what Carson had to say about Lloyd George's **Government of Ireland Bill** in the House of Commons on May 18, 1920:

> *"It has been said over and over again, 'You want to oppress the Catholic minority; you want to get a Protestant ascendancy there.' We have never asked to govern any Catholic. We are perfectly satisfied that all of them, Protestant and Catholic, should be governed from this Parliament..."*

It is precisely because Parliament since at least the 1832 Reform Bill has been dominated by the party political division between conservative and radical reform parties that it has been able to function as the protector of minorities within the United Kingdom. Because minorities have been able to participate in this political system through both its conservative and its radical wings, they have been able to secure their legitimate interests and the danger of their alienation from the state has been minimised. Scots and Welshmen have been able to function politically as Tories and Liberals and Socialists as well as nationalists, with the result that the tendency towards separatist disaffection has been offset by other more powerful tendencies. This is even true of the much newer minorities created by the arrival of immigrants from the Commonwealth. With much more scope for bitter grievances to flourish, even these minorities have been, to a considerable extent, integrated into the political life of the state through the party system. Although much remains to be done to secure their rights and abolish their grievances, the fact that they have access to the great political parties of the British system of representative government has already been enough to inhibit the development of comprehensively separatist alienation.

This was the perspective of Ulster Unionism with regard to the Catholic minority in Northern Ireland. Far from wanting to keep this minority in a state of second-class citizenship, Carson and Craig and the rest of the

Unionist leadership wanted this minority to be governed on exactly the same basis as the Protestant majority, directly from Westminster, like any other section of the British population. And if their view had prevailed, it would soon have ceased to make sense to talk in terms of a Protestant majority and a Catholic minority in Northern Ireland, since these terms would have lost their political significance as the normal British party political division established itself (or, rather, re-established itself after the hiatus of the 1886-1920 period).

The Unionists' view did not prevail. Devolved government was imposed on Northern Ireland. The nationalist tendency in the Catholic community was encouraged to maintain an attitude of separatist alienation from the institutions of the state. Nationalist local government councillors boycotted the bodies to which they had been elected. And so the system of devolved government which Westminster had foisted on Northern Ireland rapidly assumed the character of a Protestant statelet. A vicious circle had been set up from which Northern Ireland has been unable to escape. The dissolution of Stormont in 1972 offered at last the prospect of an escape. But the efforts of successive British governments since 1972 have been bent towards recreating the vicious circle. The one way out, admission to the British party political system, has been ruled out of consideration, for no good reason whatever.

British intellectuals who take to heart the evidence of discrimination against the Catholic community in Northern Ireland in the 1920 — 1972 period owe it to themselves to ponder the origins and causes of this discrimination. There is nothing mysterious or even unique about it. Wherever there is, in effect, single party rule there will be an informal system of patronage and possibly even corruption which will discriminate against those who are not associated with the party in power. Labour MPs who are inclined to moralise about the Unionist administration of Stormont should not forget the sort of things which have gone on, as a matter of course, in Tyneside and South Wales where Labour has enjoyed for decades an unshaken monopoly of local political power.

However much one may feel entitled to condemn the discrimination practised by Unionist governments against the Catholic community, it should never be forgotten that the system of devolved government which made this discrimination possible was resisted by the Unionist leadership and imposed upon them by Westminster. Nor should it be forgotten that the attitude of separatist alienation within the Catholic community since 1920 has expressed itself in a refusal to acknowledge the legitimacy of the constitutional status of Northern Ireland as a province of the United Kingdom, and has thereby furnished a considerable incentive to the practice of discriminatory patronage on the part of Unionist administrations. This attitude has been encouraged by the political representatives of the Catholic community and by the Irish Republic. But there can be no doubt that the primary responsibility for this appalling state of affairs, and for the appalling length of time for which it has persisted, rests with Westminster, and the Pontius Pilate-like postures of the mainland British parties.

CONCLUSION

Enough has been said to demonstrate that throughout its history, the attitude of the Protestant community in Northern Ireland towards the Catholic population has differed in every respect from that of the Europeans towards the Muslims of Algeria. The Protestants repeatedly supported democratic reform and, in particular, Catholic enfranchisement and emancipation; the Europeans of Algeria opposed every democratic reform in the Muslim interest. The Protestants supported the agrarian struggle of the Catholic tenant-farmers, and the Ulster Unionist movement, being based on the industrial interest instead of that of agrarian capital, supported Balfour's Land Purchase Act in 1903; the Europeans of Algeria were dominated politically by the agrarian magnates, whose interests prevailed at the expense of both the *petits blancs* and the Muslims. The Protestants have had an intimate knowledge of the Catholic population and have taken a keen interest in developments within Irish Catholicism, so that their reaction to these and related political developments have usually been thought-out and measured and often sympathetic. The Europeans of Algeria enjoyed only the most superficial contact with the Muslims, took no interest in developments within Algerian Islam, and entirely failed to notice the main developments within Muslim politics; their belated reaction to these developments was correspondingly simple-minded, hysterical and futile.

If the reader whom I have endeavoured to acquaint with these realities persists in the belief that the Protestants of Northern Ireland are straw men, a mere colonial caste without deep roots or coherence, and will therefore prove amenable to the kind of high-handed treatment which de Gaulle handed out with some success and relative impunity to the *"colons"* of Algeria, he or she must henceforth take full responsibility for this belief. It is proof against reason and evidence.

Of one thing, however, we can be sure. Only when the British government and the British media and the British political parties begin to base their attitude and their policy towards Northern Ireland upon what the Protestant community there actually is, instead of what it is mistaken for or misrepresented as, will a true, democratic and correspondingly enduring solution to the Northern Ireland problem become a political possibility.

APPENDIX
(Reproduced from "Towards Equal Citizenship",
published by the Integration Group, Belfast, September 1984.)

	Protestants %	Catholics %	Poll
Continued Direct Rule	51 72	48 79	NOP March 1974 (1) NOP March 1976 (1)
Integration	78 80 91 81 88	39 55 39 35 45	NOP March 1974 (1) NOP March 1976 (1) MORI June 1981 (2) NOP Nov. 1981 (3) NOP Feb. 1982 (3)
N. Ireland should have the same laws as the rest of the U.K.	96.6	92.2	NI Attitude Survey 1978 (4)

(1) Quoted in Studies in Public Policy No 22, Is there a concurring majority about Northern Ireland? by Richard Rose, Ian McAllister and Peter Mair, University of Strathclyde, Glasgow, 1978.

(2) Sunday Times. 18/6/81. This did not ask about the acceptability of continued Direct Rule.

(3) Polls conducted for UTV. These did not ask about the acceptability of continued Direct Rule.

(4) by E.P. Moxon-Browne and B. Boyle, May 1979.

Figures for the acceptability of 'Integration' to Roman Catholics should be read in the light of the fact that this option is universally talked about as the most extreme Unionist option. If equivalent percentages of Protestants saw a 'united Ireland' as an acceptable option, the figures would be recognised as significantly high.

Hugh Roberts is uniquely qualified to compare the political development of Northern Ireland and Algeria. He is the founder of the *Campaign for Democratic Rights for Northern Ireland*, and in his academic career he has made a special study of Algerian history and politics which involved extended stays in the country.

He received his doctorate from Oxford University for his thesis on the Kabyle Question in independent Algeria and regularly publishes articles on contemporary Algerian politics. He is Research Fellow in Political Science at the Institute of Development Studies at the University of Sussex, on sabbatical from the University of East Anglia, and is currently at work on a book on Algeria.

A former member of the Communist Party who, as President of the Oxford University Students' Representative Council, initiated and led the campaign to establish the Oxford Students' Union in 1972-3, Hugh is now active in the Labour Party. He is also Secretary of the Bevin Society, which is committed to thinking out new directions for socialist politics.